W9-BZY-187

Read what people are saying about *Living an Uncommon Life* ...

"For years, John St.Augustine has used radio as a tool to entertain, inform, and inspire countless individuals with witty, yet common-sense and informative, advice. In *Living an Uncommon Life*, John provides a blueprint for anyone seeking the ultimate truth for personal empowerment, showing how each of us is responsible for the actions we take and the ones we don't. More than anything, John confirms the fact that one person can matter and that we all make a difference in the world we live in."

—Dave Pelzer, best-selling author of
A Child Called It and Help Yourself

"From the very first show I did with John, I knew that he was a force of nature—a voice for all things possible and positive. He is a unique man—one who really walks his talk, like a modern-day Pied Piper hoping all of us will follow him to a better tomorrow. This book is a gift from a very special friend. Cherish it, for it holds the keys to a new life experience."

—Susan Ryan Jordan, best-selling
author of *The Immune Spirit*

"With *Living an Uncommon Life*, John St.Augustine brings to each page the down-to-earth, direct approach that listeners of his syndicated radio show have enjoyed for so many years. John makes it clear: Common sense does not translate to quick fix. Lasting change requires the courage to take action, and this book is your action plan if you are ready. This is certainly the most uncommon self-help book that I have read in years. Buy two copies now because you will immediately want to share it with someone you love."

—Thom Rutledge, best-selling author of
Embracing Fear and Finding the Courage to Live Your Life

"Rich with the gifts of heart and illuminating common sense, John St.Augustine brings us stories of inspiration, drawn from the lives of 'uncommon' people and his own powerful vision. Authentic, clear, and profoundly compelling, listen to his words as you read *Living an Uncommon Life*. Your life will be renewed, affirmed, and transformed."

—Cheryl Charles, Ph.D.

"*Living an Uncommon Life* is a compelling, crystal-clear jewel of a read. Verified through many notables that John has worked with over the years, it provides a solid path to live one's life at the highest, most fulfilling level. If you are ready to live the life you were sent to Earth to live, open this book and don't close it until you find yourself drifting effortlessly into the sea of infinite possibilities."

—Maureen Moss, author of *Commitment to Love: Transforming Human Nature into Divine Nature*

"The most important truths in life are the simple ones. Love, respect, hope, and service are essential ingredients for living up to your highest potential. John St.Augustine reveals the innermost workings of those who have gone within and brought forth their greatness as proof that no matter who you are, or where you are, you can begin this moment to transform your life."

—Jerry Jampolsky and Diane Cirincione, best-selling authors of *Love Is Letting Go of Fear* and *Forgiveness: The Greatest Healer of All*

"Just ask the thousands of guests John has talked to over the years about the kind of impact he has made in people's lives. I have done radio all over the country, and no one comes close to his intent, wit, and passion for people. In this book, John gives you a chance to find out what so many of us have known for years: He is an American original—positive, purposeful, and persistent. This book will change your life if you accept its wisdom!"

—Dan Clark, world-class speaker and author of *Puppies for Sale* and contributor to the *Chicken Soup for the Soul* series

Living an
UNCOMMON LIFE

ESSENTIAL LESSONS FROM
21 EXTRAORDINARY PEOPLE

JOHN ST.AUGUSTINE
Foreword by Catherine Crier

bettie youngs books

Inspiring each other with hope, possibility, and courage.

HAMPTON ROADS
PUBLISHING COMPANY, INC.

Editorial, design, and production services provided by CWL Publishing Enterprises, Inc., Madison, WI, www.cwlpub.com.

Cover design by Gina Harman
Interior illustrations © 2006 by Greg Hanson. All rights reserved.
Jerry Kramer illustration © 2006 by Diane Kramer-Magnus. All rights reserved.

Hampton Roads Publishing Company, Inc.
1125 Stoney Ridge Road · Charlottesville, VA 22902
434-296-2772 · fax: 434-296-5096
e-mail: hrpc@hrpub.com · www.hrpub.com

If you are unable to order this book from your local bookseller, you may order directly from the publisher. Call 1-800-766-8009, toll-free.

"Amazon" Words and Music © John Denver, 1991, Cherry Lane Music. Used by permission. All rights reserved.

Earl Hamner: From Walton's Mountain to Tomorrow by James E. Person Jr., Cumberland House Publishing, 2005. Used by permission of author.

The Bronx To Broadway: A Life In Show Business by Harold Thau, Applause Books 2002. Used by permission of author.

Bill Kurtis Photo by Andrew Eccles Used by permission, Kurtis Productions.

Library of Congress Cataloging-In-Publication Data
St.Augustine, John, 1958-
  Living an uncommon life : essential lessons from 21 extraordinary people / John St.Augustine.
    p. cm.
  Summary: "Nationally syndicated talk radio host John St. Augustine distills a decade of interviews with more than 5,000 guests--including Oprah Winfrey, John Denver, Walter Payton, Wayne Dyer, and others—into a roadmap for living an extraordinary life"—Provided by publisher.
  ISBN 1-57174-526-2 (6 x 9 hc : alk. paper)
  1. Conduct of life. 2. St. Augustine, John, 1958- I. Title.
BJ1581.2.S7 2006
170'.44—dc22
                                2006020609
                    ISBN 10: 1-57174-526-2 (cloth)
                  ISBN 13: 978-1-57174-526-2 (cloth)

                    10 9 8 7 6 5 4 3 2

Printed on acid-free paper in the United States

DEDICATION

For John and Carol
Sweethearts then *and* now

CONTENTS

FOREWORD

by Catherine Crier

There are countless books that tell us how to be happy or lose weight, how to succeed in business or improve our love lives. We learn steps to follow or rules to recite. There are formulas to calculate or tests to take, but few of these books tell the real secret, the actual truth behind such accomplishments.

John St.Augustine does exactly that. His inspirational life has been accomplished through action, not contemplation. With *Living an Uncommon Life*, John shares his positive "can-do experiences" and offers a plan of 21 principles for living, where success and happiness are the natural results.

John reveals the value of self-determination, of giving back to the world, and of caring about things outside our immediate lives. He teaches us to look for real solutions to problems rather than simply understanding them. He asks us to use our brains for positive, productive work, not navel-gazing reflections.

Years ago, I attended a seminar. The name of the program has become my mantra: *Freedom to Risk, Courage to Fail*. Practicing this philosophy has given me an extraordinary life. I have learned that limits are often an illusion. The process of becoming is more satisfying than simply being. The choices we make have far-reaching consequences. Most importantly, to achieve real success and happiness, we must act with integrity, respect, and love. Living these principles rather than merely feeling them makes all the difference in the world. John exemplifies these ideals. He has obtained personal success, love, and fulfillment the old-fashioned way—he has earned them. His experiences with the leaders with whom he has spent time and the personalities he interviews reveal a path that others can follow. Real success and happiness come from personal growth, meaningful contribution, and the opportunity to love and be loved by others. These are the subjects John tackles and the goals he can help us achieve. In a talk-radio world filled with low-level humor, political posturing, and voices that are bent on separating the masses, John uses his formidable presence to change lives; this simple book will do the same if you embrace the messages it contains.

Catherine Crier
New York Times best-selling author of
The Case Against Lawyers
Court TV Host of "Catherine Crier Live"

PREFACE

One hundred years ago, if you had sat in a sound-proof glass box talking to yourself for a few hours a day, chances are pretty good that men in white jackets would have escorted you to a room without windows for an extended stay. But now sitting in that booth brings with it the title of "talk radio host." Listen to most talk radio shows for any length of time and you might think that lunatics still abound, but now they are being heard *outside* the asylum. The airwaves of America are a volatile mix of political pundits, sports fanatics, and relationship gurus all spewing their own brand of conversion, information, and advice. The line between fact and fiction is blurred by the talking heads as they run each issue through their own beliefs about politics, religion, and theory.

Experience is not a qualifying factor when it comes to being behind the microphone as it relates to content. A recent *TALKERS Magazine* summit had the conservatives on one side, liberals on the other. While they batted around two issues most hotly debated these days—politics and the military—I took note of the lineup. I did some digging and discovered that out of the 37 hosts on the panel, only three had ever come close to holding a political office of any kind. (One was an aide to a former president, one held office by presidential appointment, and one was a consultant to the current governor of California.) On the military front it gets better. Four talk hosts were veterans. Of these, one had a little trouble telling the truth in front of congress, and the other is a convicted felon. The preponderance of talkers seem to know everything about everything but haven't done anything. Yet we listen as if they did.

Every day millions dial into the electronic landfill called *talk radio* with all its breaking news, urgent updates, over-the-top loudmouths, and rabid fans. The voices we listen to mirror our own beliefs and fears and give us comfort that our version of life is held by someone, somewhere, thus affirming our existence as we agree or disagree with the voice coming out of the radio. Billed as entertainment, talk radio is filled with characters, but it does little to build character during a time when that is so needed by so many.

Unless you happen to catch my show.

From the first time I sat behind the microphone and for the thousands of hours since, my underlying goal has always been the same: empowering listeners with information that cuts through the rhetoric that holds us back from living a life distinguished by success, service, and self-reliance. My program is done with humor, humility, and hope. It's done with intensity, inspiration, and insistence. It's done with passion, purpose, and power. And it's done with some of the most incredible human beings, people who have changed for the better my life and the lives of people who listen to my show.

I am following my colleagues who have written books intended to expand their base and give voice to their agenda. The only difference is that my agenda is not political and not divisive. It's all inclusive. *Life*—and all the challenges it presents—doesn't care if you are a conservative or liberal or independent, if you are straight or gay or bi. It doesn't discriminate by gender, economics, race, or religion. Either you figured out how to do life or life will do you. After my share of bumps, I've opted for figuring it out—it hurts less that way.

This book is about real-life encounters and experiences that I've had with a few of the people I've been fortunate enough to work, play, and broadcast with—those who have lived uncommon lives. Some of those profiled in this book you will know well. For others included, this will be the first time you've ever seen their names in print. All of them have taught me something. A few of them have passed on but lived so large that their imprint still affects our world. Others still here are in the process of creating their legacy. All of the folks you will read about have struggled with everything from depression to alcohol to drugs to issues of low self-esteem. I know there have been times when they wanted to give up, to throw in the towel and hide, times when the effort didn't seem worth it, and no one cared if they made it or not. We all have our demons, but we also have our angels, proven by the fact that each one of them also gave the *being within* a chance to express itself—not just the *human without*.

That really is the choice you are asked to make—how will you live your life from this point forward? *As a human being?* Or will you choose *being human?*

To merely exist in the shell we inhabit—the human part of us—is to define our existence through the external—money, cars, ring tones, homes—the drama, the chaos, and the struggle. All of the troubles the world deals with today come from the unconscious mindset that says, "What do you want from me? I'm only human!"

But that is only half correct, because as much as you are human, you are also a *being*—defined as *consciously connected* to the higher part of yourself, the place within that knows where to go, what to do, and who you are—without a shred of doubt. And that is what the people in this book are all about—*being* human.

And by doing so they learned to skate like the wind, touch millions of hearts through song and sports, endure the cruelty of captivity, and overcome abuse, built major corporations and a thousand other accomplishments. I have seen my own potential in their eyes and heard it clearer in my soul through their words. Each of them has left a mark on my life.

There is not much new in this book. Sorry, no shortcuts or bigger, faster, easier ways to get rich tomorrow and fix all your problems by the end of the week. This book is about common sense—*but common sense does not equal common practice.* If it did the world would not be in the shape it is nor would your life. Perhaps if there is one "key" to living an uncommon life, it's developing the ability to live what you already know is *right, true, and effective* and letting go of what is *wrong, false, and ineffective.*

These lessons are in no particular order—just like life. The teachers in the book come from all different backgrounds, faiths, and economic status—just like in life. And while they did not invent the concepts in the book, they do represent them in such a way as to illustrate as fully as possible the results that can be experienced by anyone who is willing to entertain the idea that our lives will expand or contract according to our thoughts and beliefs and our awareness of this fact.

In light of recent events regarding the accuracy of authors, I want to be clear that the events in the book are true and are as I remember them to be, and the lessons learned from the experiences I had—and continue to have—are really the focal point of this book. It is the message—not so much the messenger—that is most important.

—John St.Augustine
Rapid River, Michigan
Spring 2006

ACKNOWLEDGMENTS

"Thank you, thank you very much ..."

The process of writing a book is not unlike the process of making a pizza from scratch. You put out the freshest and best ingredients on the table, start with good foundation, add all the things you think will make it taste good, and then pop it into the oven. When it's cooking you have to constantly keep checking it to see if it's done. Then, after it's cooled, you put it out and, with luck, if you've followed the recipe correctly, at least one person *besides you* will think it's worth eating. The key is that it takes all right elements to pull it off. In terms of this book, I am surrounded by some of the best life has to offer.

My family has been and remains the backbone of my journey and gives me incredible support and space to do my work in the world. The love of my life, Jackie, and I have been down a lot of roads together, and she is a great life partner who keeps me in balance. Amanda and Andy are the encouragers—"Hey dad, are you going to write tonight?" Cleo the cat keeps steadfast vigil late at night while I pound the keyboard into submission. My sister Laurie and her kids, while far away in miles, are never far from my thoughts. My cousin Rich "the Sarge" Hoffman and his wife Marie have been there all my life—I deeply wish my mom and dad were here to see this.

Then there are lots of others. Mickey and Ann Skaja and the entire Skaja/Nasshan clan are incredible people who have taught me tons about overcoming the challenges of life—thanks to all of you. Bruce and Pat Hardwick and their family opened their home to us ten years ago and, in doing so, opened the doors to a whole new life. Without all of you, none of this would exist. Duane, Carol, Aaron, and Elizabeth "Lizard!" Kinnart, are my extended family and a continuous source of love and laughter.

The trip would not be the same without Dan and Cathy Creely, Ron and Jackie Eberle, Dave and Molly Stoddard, Georgie Holbrook, Marty Bethke, Tony Galbreath, and Winford Brown. Bob and Nancy Gregg encourage continually. I could not have completed this work without the lessons I have learned from Doug and Robin Hewitt and Dennis and Kathy Wotchko, and my deepest thanks to Bruce and Cindy Collins for raising such a fine son. My drive and determination were instilled a very long time ago by two very special men—Frank Preo and Ray Smith.

I want to thank the thousands of guests who have brought their incredible energy and talent to the show over the years, but most especially Jack Canfield, Mark and Patty Hansen, Les Brown, Kurt Kilpatrick, John Buccarelli, Dan Millman, Ericca Kern, Gerry Spence, Mimi Kennedy, Stacey Kumagai, Jerry Jampolosky and Diane Cirincione, Juice Newton, Barry Farber, and Roy Williams. Also included are Don Miguel Ruiz, Philippe Matthews, Susan Ryan Jordan, Judith Glaser, Linda Stouffer, Jim Bouton, Randy Hundley, Brian Kilmeade, and E.D. Hill, Dave Pelzer, Dr. Chuck Wall, Stedman Graham, Billy Ray Cyrus, John Berry, and Lisa Shaw Brawley, Dan Clark, Steve Rizzo, Royce Elliott, Tim Evans, Tom Crum, Robert White, Victoria Moran, and Ron Deutschendorf. And I cannot forget Charlie Osgood, Judge Andrew Napolitano, Scott Badenoch, Samira Rao, Dr. Cheryl Charles, Rolland Smith, and Dr. Kelly Johnson. As program producer, Ann Marie Jasso did a wonderful job of keeping the calendar filled with top-shelf guests.

My thanks to all of the publishing houses and public relations folks who keep the good stuff coming—especially Heidi Krupp and her staff in New York and Barby Bennett, who deserves a hearty "Book 'em Dano" for filling in the blanks while this book was being finished.

More than a tip of the cap to TJ Ryan, who has been one of my biggest supporters over the years and without whom my "Powerthoughts!" vignettes would not be the success they are. His editing skills and friendship have made a huge difference in the way things go. Rick Duerson deserves special thanks for making airtime a reality for my work. I deeply appreciate it. Chris and Gina Harman have been steadfast in their support and expertise for my online presence and their design of the book cover. Major kudos to Thom Rutledge, Jan Goldstoff, Megan McDonough, Jana Stanfield, Cathy Bolton, Scott Jeffrey, Robert Pino, Dr. John Powers, Lexie Brockway-Potamkin, and Anna May Sims.

The Chicago Connection keeps me moving in a good direction—my longtime friend and sounding board Ginny Weissman, high-fives to Karen Dillon, Joan Dry, and Jenniffer Weigel, Todd Musburger, Ted Albrecht, Megan Murphy, Steve Cochran, Todd Manley, Connie Payton, and Abe Thompson. A massive thank-you to the thousands of people who tune in day after day, year after year. Without you, the show doesn't exist—you are the ones that make it all work in the world.

Bettie Youngs is the earth-bound angel who believed in this book as much as I did, and it's through her faith in me that this book even exists. *Vive La France!* Susan Heim is an editor extraordinaire; her additions and subtractions make this work top shelf—literally.

Greg Hanson's illustrations captured the *spirit* of these extraordinary people. His talent and artistic gifts bring a new dimension to the words I have written, and I am honored to have his hand and heart on paper. As usual, Pat Hardwick knew whom to call when the time came to draw. Diane Kramer-Magnus created the illustration of her father Jerry Kramer, and it was at her home that the idea for illustrating the book was born.

My deepest thanks to Catherine Crier, who graciously penned the foreword for this book—her stand for personal and civic responsibility, along with her insistence that all of us make a difference, has always been a great source of inspiration and hope. Jack Jennings and the good people of Hampton Roads Publishing and Bill Gladstone brought it all together.

And, of course, to the 21 amazing, incredible, committed, and talented people who have shared and taught me so much over a lifetime and whose lessons are revealed in this work—you have helped me transform from a *human being to being human.* My thanks to all of you rest in the following words from Winfred Rhodes—*"Life's greatest achievement is the continual remaking of yourself so that at last you know how to live."*

Thanks for showing the rest of us how it's done.

CHAPTER 1

On Being Human

*Trust thyself. Every heart vibrates to that
string.*

—Ralph Waldo Emerson

I had my first inkling that my life might not go the way I expected
when I was 19 years old. On Friday January 19, 1978 at exactly
10:05 P.M. I died—at least for a moment or two. This was according to a friend of mine who gave me a couple of sharp smacks to
the chest that got my heart going again. I was working part time for a
major drug store chain, and my job was working with the bailing
machine, crushing cardboard boxes into hay-bale-size blocks. The
machine had been malfunctioning, so we were using the button inside
the fuse box to initiate the cycle. The last thing I remember was press-
ing that button with my right thumb and holding the iron door closed
with my left hand. Then there was a deep *humming* sound and the
strangest thought came to mind—*I'm dead.*

Somehow I was able to pull myself off the machine. My right hand
looked like someone used it for target practice. My skin was so hot it
was blue. The eyelets blew out of my shoes, and the buttons burned
off my shirt. The pharmacist on duty (who just happened to stay late

that night) found me. I remember his name was Mike. He was a Vietnam veteran. He took my pulse and found nothing. He proceeded to pound my chest and give me CPR until the paramedics came. He saved my life.

On that night, it just so happened that Chicago Fire Department ambulance #32 was only a few blocks away, and the next thing I knew they were hooking me up to monitors and IV lines and lifting me onto a stretcher. My parents came to the emergency room in record time, and there was some discussion if my right hand could be saved. My dad convinced the attending doctor that someday I would need that hand, and so they painstakingly cut away the dead and burned skin and bandaged me up the best they could.

By midnight I was in a room with my bandaged right hand hanging from a hook to keep the swelling down. The stench of burnt flesh permeated everything. I lay there wondering what in the world was going on. How did this happen to me?

Still, every so often we discover that what we *need* and what we *want* are two very different things.

A few days later, a nurse was teaching me how to clean and scrub the burns on my hand, a very painful process. The second- and third-degree burns were horrible to look at, and I begged her to do it for me. "John," she said to me, "the moment you take ownership of the pain is the moment you begin to heal." Since that day, those words have applied to every area of my life.

I would go on to manage my healing. I underwent plastic surgery and skin grafts on my hand and then, being the bulletproof age of 20, I believed my life had had its bad turn and from then on everything would be just fine. After watching the Iran hostages paraded on TV in 1980, I fully intended to join the Marines. Therefore, a few days later I went to the recruiting office, but the Marines were out to lunch. However, the Coast Guard recruiter in the next office was just as happy to see me. I signed on the dotted line and spent the years 1980 to 1984 in the aviation wing of the Coast Guard, that overlooked branch of the Armed Forces, with responsibility for search-and-rescue missions. Semper Paratus! These remain some the proudest years of my life.

After an honorable discharge from the Guard, I had no real plan for my life. However, things started to happen quickly, thanks to a blond-haired, blue-eyed girl named Jackie.

I met Jacqueline Marie Skaja in the fall of 1984 and fell head over heels in love. We married in May of 1986. Now I had a great job, a smart (and very pretty) wife, and the future seemed secure. Well, perhaps you know the phrase, when everything seems to be going right, that's when things go wrong.

Just two weeks after Jackie and I got married, we were driving home from the Chicago suburbs after picking up our wedding pictures. It was a beautiful spring evening. Suddenly a drunk driver ran a red light with his Cadillac and hit our 1983 Pontiac Firebird broadside at nearly 60 miles per hour as I was legally driving though the intersection. Our car folded like an accordion. I took the brunt of the impact on my left side. My knees and legs went up into the dash and my right hand—the same one that was hurt before—went through the windshield. The car spun in a circle, spewing metal and glass everywhere.

I heard Jackie screaming. I saw our photo album lying in the highway, and my last conscious thought was "Not again. I'm too young to die." Then everything went dark.

Rescue workers—many of whom I knew personally—covered me up while they started to pry the mangled car apart. A nurse who was at the scene checked my pulse and thought I would make it, but she wasn't sure. Then, as if by some weird remote control, I was wide awake under the tarp and could hear everything. I was hypersensitive to the sound of metal being cut, the smell of gasoline on the hot pavement, the sobs of my wife—I could *feel* what was going on, even though I could *see* none of it. Strange as it may sound, I felt fully alive.

The minute the workers cut the door from its hinges, I popped up from under the tarp like a jack-in-the-box. I was ready to walk home— about 20 miles. Adrenaline had kicked in big time. The rescuers calmed me down—amazed I was even alive—and put me in the ambulance for a short ride to the ER. Amazingly, I went home that night with only bruises and a bad cut on the hand. Other than that, I was OK. Or so I thought.

Two months later I was sitting in a scorching hot courtroom and finally locked eyes with the man who had hit us. He received a slap on the wrist for running the light (he left the scene of the accident but turned himself in two days later). There was no charge of drunk driving even though he had priors. I went home that night full of rage. Shortly after midnight, that rage exploded in the form of anxiety attacks so severe that my wife called both her parents and the police. When the police showed up, they were convinced I was in some drug-induced rage and took me to the hospital. Waves of anger swept through me, and there was nothing I could do to stop it. In short order I was sent down to a "facility" on Lake Shore Drive in Chicago where really big guys in white jackets took away my belt, shoelaces, and pocketknife. I was in a room with a guy who talked to the chair next to his bed like it was a dog. I can still hear him ... "Sit ... Sit ... Sit." I thought this guy was wacko—*and they thought I was, too.*

After a couple of days of observation, the doctor assigned to my case unraveled the mess: *too much pressure on the nervous system in too short of a time—getting married, smashed in an accident, off work for a couple of months, person causing accident gets off scott-free, John implodes.* I got a private room and more time alone. Jackie had thoughts about divorcing me, and I would not have blamed her. It got worse before it got better. The doctor prescribed Xanax, a powerful drug for anxiety disorders. He told me that anxiety comes out differently in people. For me it was almost like "The Incredible Hulk" metamorphosis: calm one minute, then something would set me off, and *bam,* I was crushing full cans of Coke without opening them. This is not to mention a few side effects of the drug. Some I learned of were release of hostility and other paradoxical effects such as irritability and hallucinations. Just what I needed—something to add fuel to the fire that burned inside me.

Einstein's been quoted as saying the thinking that creates a problem cannot be the thinking that solves the problem. I had to find a way to harness the powerful feelings that were surging inside me and make them work for me, not against me. The words came back: *When you take ownership of the pain, you begin to heal.* It had worked for me physically, but what about mentally? I decided to stop taking the drug and began to find little mental games to play when I felt the anxiety well up, like picturing a barbell in my mind. I would bend but never break. In the beginning it was tough; I really felt the weight. But gradually I gained control over my thoughts, and the weight became easier and easier to handle.

To demonstrate how anxious I was, for *one year* Jackie and I slept on a mattress on the floor with the lights on in the living room of our small apartment. How we made it through that first year truly amazes me—not the best way to start a marriage. Still we must have done a few things right—we recently celebrated our 20th year together.

Through this experience, I began to learn that the mind is our most powerful tool for dealing with any experience, but most of us never learn to master our thoughts or harness our true potential. That automobile accident turned out to be a teacher in disguise, providing an opportunity for me to grow. It was time for me to start on a new path.

Just a few short years later, with a college degree under my belt and a baby girl named Amanda added to the family, our lives found a bit of normalcy. I was a substitute teacher at the high school I had attended and was working with pro athletes in my other career as a sports marketing consultant. In January of 1991, our second child, Andy, joined our family. I thought for sure the hard times were behind us. Not quite yet.

Amanda was born with a kidney defect, and by the time she was five her right kidney had become toxic and had to be removed. We were devastated. I can remember watching her ride the gurney into the operating room sitting up like *a big girl* with Teddy by her side and then the nerve-wracking hours that followed. After a successful surgery, we rushed into the recovery room where she lay and held her close. Bathed in the glow of the monitors, I began to wonder, "How did all this happen in my life? I've been out of high school for just over ten years!"

For the time being, Amanda's prognosis was good, but she would eventually need a kidney transplant. She rebounded and did well for a long time. Not long after the surgery I found myself in the deal of a lifetime, which would later turn out to be the turning point of a lifetime. The details really don't matter, but in the middle of the deal I was asked to give a commencement address at a high school in Upper Michigan, a place I had visited once and thought of more as a part of Canada than the United States. It was hardly a place I would think of ever living. I accepted the invitation, and we drove from Chicago to the Upper Peninsula, the UP, as it's called. I was overwhelmed to see an entire town attend a graduation for just 27 young people. I half expected Andy and Barney to pull up in the Mayberry patrol car! They had brought me in to tell the grads how to be "successful," but the lesson went in reverse—it was me who learned that success meant community, the support and faith in the future demonstrated by the loving parents, teachers, and neighbors in attendance.

As if by the design of the universe, I was confronted by the proverbial fork in the road: one road meant staying in Chicago and battling my way through a business deal that I knew deep down wasn't going to work, which was going to cost me big time in terms of friendship and money. Or the other road, which meant following that still, small voice inside and trying something new. I chose to take that second road.

Bruce and Pat Hardwick own a small, ten-room motel in Rapid River, Michigan, and their son Tom was in the class to whom I spoke on graduation. We had become fast friends, and they offered my family a place to live. So it came to pass that on one fall day in 1996 the Hardwicks, with a horse trailer in tow, led a caravan from Michigan to our front door, and in just hours we were packed and heading north, leaving Chicago behind.

My family and I began living in the same motel I had stayed in just months earlier as "Mr. Successful." I sure didn't feel very successful. As a matter of fact, I felt that by moving to this small town in upper Michigan, I had possibly ruined my life—not to mention the lives of my wife and kids. There I was at the age of 37, an adult male with a college degree living in a motel. It was at an all-time low—or so I thought. All during this period, I had a recurring dream of myself as a backpacker walking on the side of a curved road lined with pine trees and the sun slowly setting. I took it as a sign that I should get my gear together and get moving. However, it was to be much more than that.

Two weeks after we moved and put the kids in school, Jackie found a job. (She is an incredible floral designer.) We put our household goods in storage and settled into the kitchenette-rooms 9 and 10 at the Hillcrest Motel. I had the dream again. I decided to share this with Bruce, an Ojibway fire-keeper and very respected wise man. He took my hand and led me to the back of his property near the tree line and told me that he believed it was time for me to go on a "vision quest" and that my whole life had led me to this point—or I could choose to go back to the life I had led before. He was crying as he spoke the words, and I somehow knew it was the truth. I wanted to find a new direction for my life. I was tired of getting hit with the spiritual two-by-four. I needed to find the purpose for my existence.

That evening Bruce lit a sacred fire, and I announced to the people—most of whom I hardly knew—that I was to embark on a walk from Rapid River to Chicago (from where we had just moved) *and back*. There was silence in the lodge and then a man with silver hair down to his waist, Duane Kinnart, stood up and said, "I will be going with you" in such a matter-of-fact voice that it seemed perfect. I had no plans or provisions, no job, no sense of why this had to be done, but I knew I had to walk. Through some amazing connections, a young man, who was related to Bruce's wife, Pat, heard about the journey, and soon 20-year-old Joe Johnson became the third musketeer.

We walked out of that lodge a few days later and made it all of 19 miles the first day. The next morning, we had to help each other out of bed. My father-in-law, Mickey, backed up the walk in his van. I was convinced at the time he did so because he thought I was crazy, but his presence on the trip was invaluable.

The walk itself is another book, but I have to say that I don't know a more spiritually grounded man than Duane. It seemed that he was waiting for me to arrive as a puzzle piece for his own journey. His presence is an example that all of us, especially men, can not only change, but can entirely reroute our primitive energies and, by doing so, create a life that is of the highest order. We made it to Chicago in four weeks. Then, Duane and Joe headed home with their families. I stayed back. The real journey for me was about to begin. I started walking again.

As I proceeded, alone for the first time in my life—really alone—I was somehow able to connect with my true self, the one who exists past all the pain and worry that corrodes the human spirit during a lifetime. My steps got lighter, my thoughts went higher, and I began to put back together the pieces of myself that life had knocked out of place. At one point, in Kettle Moraine State Park in Wisconsin, I took everything out of my wallet except the cash and burned it all—pictures, IDs, you name it—so as to symbolically strip away who I used to be.

Not long after that and just past a small Wisconsin town, as I was keeping a pretty good pace, hoping to make it to a designated point where I would connect with a friend to clean up a bit, I found myself walking on the side of that tree-lined road with a backpack just as the sun was beginning to set. I froze in place. This could not be happening. It was the same place I had seen in my dreams for the past six months. That moment blew away any vestiges of what had constituted reality for me.

I just stood there ... and then a thought leapt to mind: *Go on the radio.*

That made about as much sense as living in a motel or walking to Chicago or being stuck to a bailing machine or getting hit by a drunk driver. I had no previous interest in radio or knowledge of that field, but what the heck—it seemed like some kind of divine order, and I was in no position to argue.

Bruce followed me in his car the last week of the walk—and it was on a 30-mile trek in one day (up to then, I had been doing about 15 miles or so a day) that I knew the walk was over. It was late fall, and as I trudged north along Highway M-35 with Bruce behind me in his blue Dodge, I found that the only places I could see to put my feet were illuminated by the headlights of Bruce's car.

At that moment, I had a strange "Celestine Prophecy" moment. While I knew full well the road was being lit by an automobile's headlights, it looked as if the light emanated from me. I thought, "Where I go, the light goes. If I don't choose to let it shine through me, the path is dark. When I allow it to guide my way, my steps are certain." I stopped on the dark road and collapsed like a pile of laundry. Bruce helped me back into the car.

The next morning as he went ahead to get coffee, I walked in a snow squall and made it about three miles before wandering off the road and into the woods. I lay down in the snow and let myself go. I have no idea how long I was there, but a few inches of accumulation gave a hint. I eventually got up and made my way back to the highway and found Bruce waiting for me. He insisted that we go back and look at the spot I had chosen to lie down. About 30 yards from the road was a perfect outline of my body in the snow. As we stood there looking, Bruce noticed that the whole of the ground was pure white except the area where my heart would be. There it was green from the grass underneath.

My heart had been reborn. One life ended and another began. We both stood crying as if at a funeral. The vision quest was complete. It was the day before Thanksgiving 1996. I returned to the little motel and slept for three days.

After the revelation about going on the radio, I thought everything would just drop into place. It wasn't that simple. It took almost a year—August of 1997 to be exact—for the opening to reveal itself. I called several radio stations about an idea of doing a show that would inspire people without reverting to the religious, a show that would encourage people and help them find common ground by being uncommon. Every person I talked to turned me down. ("No one is going to listen to you" is not the thing to say to a guy from Chicago who is living in a motel calling radio stations out of the phone book in his underwear.) Finally, however, Alice Sabuco, the general manager of WDBC in Escanaba, Michigan, gave me a chance.

I had five shows to prove it could work. The first four were less than stellar, but the fifth one, featuring Stedman Graham, who is well-known as the best friend of Oprah Winfrey, but also an author, speaker, and businessperson (we had played golf together and I had done some speaking for his Athletes Against Drugs organization), was a hit. The phone lines lit up, and I was off to the races.

That was nine years ago.

Since that day I have hosted over 8,000 shows, been honored by the Michigan Association of Broadcasters as the best talk host three times, and have interviewed over 5,000 people from all walks of life. So much for people not wanting to hear about the possibilities that life has to offer.

It turned out to be a good thing I decided to take that walk, because I found a new life waiting for me. And so was my daughter Amanda—or more specifically waiting for my kidney. In July 2002 the wizards and angels at University of Wisconsin Children's Hospital in Madison placed my kidney in Amanda's 13-year-old body, and I had the rare gift of giving one of my children life for the second time. It's now four years later, and she shines with perfect health.

After the surgery, I took nine weeks off from the show. Then, after much soul-searching, I decided I really needed a break. So on New Year's Eve 2002 I signed off, not knowing if I would ever return. It turned out to be a 33-month hiatus—with some of my time off spent working on the book you hold in your hands. I returned to radio on September 12, 2005. While it took a little time to knock off the rust, I felt better than ever about the messages and lessons I believe the world needs to hear. I knew there had to be an alternative to the grade-school talk show radio behavior and mentality that fills the airwaves these days, and that's what I wanted my voice to stand for.

The words I've put down in this book are just scratching the surface of my life. There have been a million tears and just as many laughs. I have stumbled and fallen more times than I care to remember, but each time, I've gotten up and, with each lesson, I learn that the falling hurts less and the getting up comes faster.

Much of how my life is today is not what I ever thought it could or would be. I am not yet 50 and both my parents are gone. When I see my daughter in a bathing suit at our annual excursion to Clear Lake and see that long scar down her flank and across her belly, I remember that a part of *me* resides in *her*. And while thousands of people tune in every day to get my take on the world, I sometimes still see myself as Augie, the skinny blond-haired kid who hung out at Belding Playground with Al, Rich, Jimmy, Bubba, and Menz, not an award-winning talk radio host. But in a very real sense the things that have taken me the furthest in life I learned on the streets of Chicago, on the ball fields, and in the backyards with my buddies. We looked out for each other. We knew each other's families. We were curious about our lives. We worked together as a team, and we had hope about the future—and still do.

As I conclude this chapter, I want to stress that while my life has had its ups and downs—as yours surely has as well—we should remember that everything that happens to us is a learning experience that gets us more in touch with our humanity and our virtually unlimited potential. The fact is that it's all a matter of perspective and choice. I can easily focus on all the things that didn't go the way I wanted them to or the utter chaos I caused when I acted out of my lower self or played the victim role. Or I can remember to turn the microscope on myself, check out the places that I need to shore up, and get about the business of living the short time I have at a much higher level of service, joy, and purpose. It's just a matter of understanding what makes the most sense for living a fulfilled life.

* * *

As I near the half-century mark, the reality sets in that it's possible I have more yesterdays than tomorrows, and after surviving some very uncommon events in life, there seems to be an urgency for me to squeeze every moment for all it's worth. The smallest event is cause for celebration. As I write these words, sunlight streams through the window, illuminating my face with the last rays of the setting sun. The birds are still busy going about their business, and Cleo the cat watches them scurry across the lawn in search of bugs, occasionally growling under her breath. Peeper frogs are beginning to clear their throats for a full night of singing, and even though it's summer, the air is beginning to cool. Shortly the sun will set and give way to darkness, and the ancient cycle will be set in motion and to witness it one more time is a gift. Being alive is a very good thing.

I have truly led an uncommon life, some of it by choice, other times by chance when it seemed the universe was keeping me on my toes just to make sure I stay balanced. I look back on the journey and can pinpoint the events on the path that were turning points—the severe electrical injury at 19, the auto accident at 27, walking nearly one thousand miles at 37, donating a kidney at 43, and now sharing this journey with the world in this book at 47. While I don't suggest you stick your finger in a wall socket or take a whack from a drunken driver, I do recommend that you take whatever time you have left on your lifetime warranty and put it to some good use. When it's all said and done and you reach for your last breath, you can rest well in knowing that you have lived an uncommon life and by doing so given permission for others to do the same. There is no better time than now and no one better to do it than you.

CHAPTER 2

Your Voice Matters

O, how wonderful is the human voice! It is
indeed the organ of the soul!
—Henry Wadsworth Longfellow

I simply stood in the doorway and cried. My clothes were soaked from the pouring rain on this cold, raw autumn morning, and the words tumbled out of my mouth like puzzle pieces falling on the floor. "John Denver died," I sobbed to my wife. "He's gone."

We had just moved into the house the day before, and the cable TV was not yet connected so I had not heard the news until driving the kids to school that morning. After living in a motel for a year, life was beginning to turn around—and now *this*. I felt like a mule had kicked me in the head. I spent the next hour trying to pull myself together for the show that morning. The last thing I ever thought I would do is a tribute to the man whose voice had reached into my soul as a young person and whose music, message, support, and eventual friendship had been such an integral part of my life.

For millions of people around the world, John Denver needs no introduction. He stepped into the spotlight during the folk days of the turbulent '60s with the Chad Mitchell Trio and penned "Oh Babe, I

Hate to Go," which became "Leaving on a Jet Plane" at the urging of producer Milt Okun. Peter, Paul, and Mary recorded the song, and it launched Henry John Deutschendorf Jr. into a solo career the likes of which few entertainers can claim. His soaring tenor voice and simple yet profound lyrics struck a chord in the '70s, and you could hardly go ten minutes without hearing, "Country Roads," "Rocky Mountain High," or "Annie's Song" on the radio—to the delight of millions of fans and the consternation of critics.

While he was labeled by music reviewers as "The Mickey Mouse of Rock & Roll," the folks who mattered most to John—real people in need of hope and inspiration—understood his message. When the seventies ended, no one in the world had sold more albums. John Denver stands as one of the all-time best-selling solo artists, with worldwide sales of over 75 million albums. He racked up 21 gold, 14 platinum, and 7 multi-platinum certified albums without pyrotechnics, dance routines, or overblown stage productions—just a guitar and his voice. In 1993, he was the first nonclassical artist to receive the prestigious Albert Schweitzer Music Award—*"For a life's work dedicated to music and devoted to humanity."*

His considerable catalog of songs and ability to communicate with people from all walks of life led to his induction into the Songwriter's Hall of Fame in 1996. Not bad for a guy who learned to play songs on a 1910 Gibson F-Hole Jazz guitar that his grandmother gave him as a gift at the age of 12.

John's music clearly reflects the conscience of a concerned citizen, a man working for the improvement of the quality of life for all people—environmentally, socially, and politically. He was asked to serve as a member of the Presidential Commission on World and Domestic Hunger and was one of the five founders of The Hunger Project—an organization committed to the sustainable end of chronic hunger. John was asked to be a member of the fact-finding delegation that toured African countries devastated by drought and starvation as a representative of The Hunger Project and UNICEF. Because of his tireless effort and dedication, President Ronald Reagan awarded John with the Presidential "World Without Hunger" Award. Long before today's entertainers were talking about the plight of those in need, John Denver was singing to the four corners of the world about hunger, environmental responsibility, and the cultivation of the human spirit as salvation from our incessant need to destroy not only each other, but the planet as well.

Perhaps his biggest contributions came in the form of The Windstar Foundation, created with Tom Crum and Hal Thau in 1976. Located in Snowmass, Colorado, it was designed as a nonprofit "think tank" focused on creating a sustainable future, and in 1992 he launched the Plant-It-2020 program that has planted nearly one million indigenous trees since its inception.

John was the catalyst for the "Citizens in Space" program and hoped to be aboard the first flight—but in a twist of fate, that seat went to a schoolteacher named Christa McAuliffe onboard the ill-fated Challenger in 1986. His commitment and contribution to wilderness preservation and his support for groups ranged from the National Wildlife Federation to the Cousteau Society. While his time was a far-too-short 53 years, his voice echoes two lifetimes worth of service, contribution, and commitment to a brighter and more sustainable future for humanity and the importance of planting your feet firmly on the Earth and making your voice count for what you believe in.

I did the best I could with the show that day, but it was the longest two hours of radio I had ever done. I spoke with the executive director of the Windstar Foundation, and shared a few stories about John that had made such a difference in my life and the world. The morning was a blur, and, once home, I cried on and off all day—not only because the Earth had lost its troubadour, but because a piece of me went down in that plane, too.

For the longest time I could not put my finger on exactly what John's music touched in me. It was more than just an appreciation of nature or the simplicity of life on a farm or the wonder of the ocean depths. And then one day the answer came to me: Denver's music gave me a sense of *belonging* ... that my presence here was not happenstance, and that somehow the world was a better place because I was in it. If there is one great hurdle humans must overcome, it is the belief that we are some kind of cosmic mistake. John's music changed all that for me because it awakened within me that spark we all have, but often do everything in our power to extinguish—the spark of *spirit* that gives birth to our *voice*. At the moment all this came to me, I recalled a meeting I had had with

John that could only be described as a "divine intersection" on both our parts. It was the conversation that put in place the first steps I would take on my way to my life's work in radio.

On a late November night in 1992, I was watching *The Tonight Show* with Jay Leno, half asleep on the couch, when Leno came back after commercials and announced, "You all know my next guest. He is an amazing singer/songwriter, an old friend who will be appearing at the Wang Center in Boston on December third. Ladies and gentlemen, John Denver." As John launched into his first song, I did not hear a word. I had this overwhelming feeling that I needed to be in Boston, for some unknown reason, on December third, just a couple of weeks away. It was strange, to be sure. I had first met John back in 1980 at a fundraiser in Colorado, and then at various Windstar Symposia over the years. In 1989, he performed a one-man show called "Higher Ground" in Chicago, and that night we spoke at length about environmental responsibility and the human condition. After growing up and listening to his music, meeting John and getting to know him a bit was more than I had ever expected. But this was different. I had never been to Boston in my life, but the message was clear . . . *just go.*

I landed at Logan Airport and took a cab to a motel ten miles or so from downtown Boston—a small, nameless place near the ocean. As I unpacked my suitcase, I thought to myself, *Now what?* I had no tickets to the concert, no idea of why I was there, and no way of finding out if John would even have time to talk! I thought for a moment about forgetting the whole thing, but decided to follow through since I was already there. I pulled out the phone book and scanned the hotel listings. After a half-dozen calls or so, I found Kris O'Connor, John's road manager. Kris was great. Did I need a ticket? How much time did I need? Did I know how to get to the concert from where I was? Kris said that John would have about 20 minutes or so to talk before they began the sound check and asked if that would be all right. Considering I had no idea what we were going to talk about, it sounded fine to me.

The cabdriver dropped me off a few blocks from the Wang Center, and I walked through a nearby park filled with people getting ready for Christmas. Real chestnuts were roasting, and lovers rode in horse-drawn carriages in the gently falling snow. It was a scene right out of

Currier and Ives. While I walked, I thought about what I was going to say to John, but all that came to mind was the work I had been doing in Chicago—speaking with students and teachers about environmental awareness and responsibility. I had grabbed a handful of letters when I left home, written to me by students, parents, and others about the impact of those talks. They were stuffed in my coat pocket, but even that subject seemed too small to fly all the way to Boston.

I checked into the theater a few minutes before the time Kris and I had agreed on and waited in the security area. Forty-five minutes later, the door popped open, and there were John and James Burton, his guitar player, followed by O'Connor. All were covered in snow, obviously late, and not in the best of moods.

Denver looked a little surprised to see me sitting there, but he nodded and said, "Hey, John. What are you doing here? This isn't Chicago, pal," and then he kept walking. Kris walked over and said, "We lost our window to talk because we are running late. John can't meet with you. I am really sorry. But here is a ticket to the show, and you can wait down in the office while the guitars get tuned until it starts." *Not as sorry as I am*, I thought. *This must have been all a big mistake.* Somehow my wires must have gotten crossed, and I should have stayed home.

I sat in the inner sanctum of the Wang Center while Denver rehearsed above me on the stage with a children's choir for the show. Kris checked in on me and offered all he could—a cheeseburger. "I have some extra cheeseburgers in the bag if you want one," he said. I sat munching on the burger, and as I listened to them tune up, that feeling came over me again: *We have to talk.*

With cheeseburger in hand, I climbed up to the stage area and stood in the wings watching John and the band do their thing. Kris noticed me and walked over.

"Where are you guys performing tomorrow night?" I asked.

"Pittsburgh. Why?"

"Then I will see you there. John and I gotta talk. That's all I know."

Kris sighed and said, "Meet us back at the room you were just in after the show. You'll have five minutes at most."

Off I went to the main entrance to stand in line with the 5,000 other people who were coming to the show, seeking refuge from the bitter winter evening to find warmth in the man and his music. The concert was an incredible two-and-a-half-hour affair with John in fine voice, and at one point I thought I could feel the seats shaking when he hit the high note in "O Holy Night." Two curtain calls later—and I'm sure a lot of money raised for Catholic Charities of Boston—the theater slowly emptied out. I made my way backstage. As I came down the hallway, John was sipping a cup of tea and talking to an elderly couple. I waited, leaning on the wall, feeling very much like I should turn around and leave. Whatever needed to be said could wait for another time. Then, I heard that familiar voice.

"Hey, John."

"Hey, John back."

We shook hands. One thing I will never forget is that when John Denver talked to you, he was totally with you. You had his undivided attention, and he looked straight into your eyes.

"Kris says you flew here from Chicago to talk ... about what?"

Here we go. "I, uh ... have no idea really."

"Excuse me?"

"Well, I just had this overwhelming feeling that I needed to be here. So I jumped on a plane and ... here I am. I thought that somehow maybe you would know."

There was an awkward silence.

"Did you bring me something?" he asked.

I started to say no ... and then I remembered the letters. "Yeah, I did. I brought you some letters to read. They are thoughts and thanks from some of the kids I spoke to and ideas they have for making a difference in the world."

Denver looked over a couple of the letters with that big grin of his, and slowly nodded his head up and down as if to say yes.

He looked up at me—and said something that changed my life.

"John, you have the opportunity to become an important player in the world game by living up to your talent for connecting with people. You speak it ... I sing it ... it's the same thing. You are the only one who can do what you came here to do. *Your voice can make a huge difference in the way things go.* I know that the coming years are going to prove me right."

I stood there with my mouth open and tears welling up in my eyes. He put his hand on my shoulder, looked me in the eyes, and said, *"You are a gift to the world."*

I had nothing to say.

I had flown all the way to Boston for a message that it was time for me to hear from a source I could not ignore.

"Hey, put those letters in my bag, and I will read them on the way home. Maybe I can learn something from those kids. And I am sorry you had to wait all night. You need a ride back to the hotel?"

Still somewhat stunned, I mumbled that I would be fine.

"I have to run—there is a press thing upstairs. You'll put those letters in my bag before you leave, right?" We were shaking hands now, arms stretched to the max—John going one way, me another. "You stay in touch."

"I will."

The letters made it into the bag. I found my way back to the motel and was home in Chicago by the next afternoon. When my wife asked me what happened, I had little to say. "Not really sure." But I knew what had happened. Someone told me the truth, and for the first time in my life I knew it. It's the kind of truth that hits you like a two-by-four in the back of the head—it both wakes you up and knocks you down. It takes time to recover and find your bearings.

Six months later, I received a call from the Windstar Foundation. It seems Mr. Denver brought those letters to a board meeting and wanted to know how they could implement a program that touched city people the way that I was. I sent them my outline and left it at that. I felt that the trip to Boston was now valid, and that was the end of it.

But it was just the beginning.

Two years later, the phone rang on a bright August morning—as I was cleaning out the litter box, of all things—and it was one of those *answer this!* rings. I dropped my all-important duties and picked it up. It was the Windstar folks from Colorado. "Dr. Mae Jemison cancelled at the last minute for the ninth annual Choices for the Future Symposium. John would be forever grateful if you would come and speak in Aspen for the event. He says you have a real gift for bringing people together, and your voice needs to be heard."

Again, I was stunned. *Forever grateful? You've got to be kidding me.*

Jokingly, I said I would check my calendar—and, of course, the dates were open. My wife Jackie and I flew out to Colorado, and on a sunny Saturday morning I found myself looking at a sea of faces in the Aspen Music Tent and talking about the importance of claiming your heritage and place in The Human Family. On that day, my life changed again—not just because of the faith John had in me, but the faith I remembered in myself. It's the faith that says I have a right for my voice to be heard, and that right comes with a responsibility for me to live up to all that I am capable of being. I had found my voice.

That was over ten years ago.

So very much has changed since then. Instead of talking to students at schools, I now have the opportunity to be a part of thousands of people's lives every day on radio—using the microphone as John used his guitar—as an extension of my higher self. The words he spoke to me have all come true—not just because I believed them, but because I *knew* they were true. I am not sure what path I would have taken if John had not been such a strong reminder to me about living up to my talents and gifts. It is a sobering truth to realize that what you see in another, you also possess yourself—for better or for worse—but this truth is of no use unless we act upon the gifts we have been given and use them to elevate ourselves and those around us.

When the news of the day heads into the realm of the ridiculous, or the juggling act of husband, father, and radio guy gets to be a bit much, I do what I have always done: sit back, drop in one of John's CDs, and let the music remind me of what I am here for and what is possible. His voice, in all its incredible clarity and range, fills the room with images of a better way of being—wild places that offer refuge for the human spirit and how utterly important it is that we claim our gifts and offer them to each other. Then everything becomes clear, and I hear him saying, *"John, your voice can make a huge difference in the way things go . . ."*

It is, perhaps, the most important lesson we need to remember.

Let this be a voice for the mountains
Let this be a voice for the rivers
Let this be a voice for the forests
Let this be a voice for the flowers
Let this be a voice for the oceans
Let this be a voice for the deserts
Let this be a voice for the children
Let this be a voice for the dreamers
Let this be a voice of no regret

—John Denver

"Amazon" Copyright © 1991 Cherry Lane Music
Used by permission, Cherry Lane Music

Finding Your Own Voice

It does not take much research to come to the conclusion that most of us have forgotten our voice, which is one of our greatest gifts. The headlines are filled with people living out the *effects* of their life, not the *cause*. Most of us have fallen into a slow but sure descent from the hope and joy of living we once knew to a mediocre experience where we do the same things over and over and expect life to be different. We spend countless hours watching reality shows on TV, while the most important reality show—*our lives*—slips by unnoticed. We get busy with the kids, the job, and the bills—forgetting that there will *always* be the kids, the job, and the bills—but that life is one thing you will eventually run out of.

Any good personal-fitness trainer will tell you that the most important exercises you can do to strengthen the body are core movements. Focusing on movement that makes the central part of you stronger pulls it all together physically—and life is no different. At the core of your existence are your gifts—those talents and expressions that make you unlike the six billion other humans with whom you share the planet. I am not quite sure when we decide that bringing our gifts to the world isn't worth the trouble. It could be around the age of 12, when we have heard the word "no" thousands of times. Or by age 14, when we have witnessed so much of the world chaos that the media sends our way. Or maybe we're the products of the old "children should be seen and not heard" way of thinking. Somewhere in all of this and countless other moments, we lose sight of our core gifts and allow the erosion of life to silence us. We settle for less than we can be and become mute to the challenges we face in the twenty-first century.

The truth, however, remains unchanged—no matter what "circumstances" or "effects" you have experienced or endured. I learned long ago that "challenges" are there, in fact, to drive you inward—to your core—and the gifts you have forgotten. *Webster's Dictionary* defines a "gift" as "a notable capacity, talent or endowment that is given voluntarily without thought to compensation." Ironically, though, if you focus on your gifts, the odds are that someone will eventually compensate you for your notable capacity and talent. That compensation comes in many forms, and once you recognize your core gifts and align your life with them, you become a magnet for everything and everyone in the world that is a part of your talent. "Voice" is defined as "the ability to convey emotion, feeling or power." It is the only sound humankind has that can affect another solely by vibration, intent, and command.

But none of this matters if you have bought into the lie that you really don't matter, or that things are the way they are and there is nothing *you* can do to change them. Or even worse—that you are somehow a mistake, and your existence is some kind of "cosmic burp." The fact is, the odds of just being born are astronomical. Either everything in the universe had to line up just right for you to get here, or you were born just waiting to die. It's your choice, and how you use your voice will reflect on how you see the life you have been given.

I am asking you to give it one more shot—make a commitment to find that core, to allow your gifts to surface and find your voice. It's easy to forget why we are here, and that living a significant life is within our reach and literally in our hands. Sometimes we need to be reminded— like John did for me—that true human evolution is about becoming all we were meant to be so we can encourage others to do the same and be the change we wish to see in the world. Sometimes it happens when we least expect it and right when we need it. When it happens, you will never be the same again, and you will remember who you are.

So how do you follow John's lead by identifying your gifts and finding your voice? I suggest the following steps.

Make a List

The human mind cannot hold two opposing thoughts at once, but being the efficient machine that it is, it sure tries to! Trying to just sit and think of your gifts is difficult, but this can be overcome by following the first rule of internal excavation at any level—when in doubt, write it out. Somewhere buried among the billions of neurons, syntaxes, and brain cells is your gift. Take out a sheet of paper and simply draw a line down the middle. On top of the first column write the word "Effort." Under that heading list everything you do that takes effort in your life—paying bills, your job, cleaning up after the kids—whatever comes to mind. Label the next column "Effortless" and begin to list the things you do that come easily—painting, gardening, your job (some things can be on both lists), restoring vintage cars—whatever comes to mind.

The purpose of this little exercise is threefold. First and foremost, you have to make a connection to your mind in a new way—outside of the usual bombardment. By writing these things down, you are going "online" and connecting to your internal Internet. Second, once you begin to identify the things that take effort, you can recognize where you are spending your energy and why. Third, the same goes for identifying the things that you do well—those things you enjoy that take little effort. Writing this list is like opening the floodgates. Once you have written down everything that comes to mind (and it could take some time, so put on the coffee), ask yourself this question, "Is there more?" And watch what happens. Then write it down. Just when you think you have reached the end of the list, you are really just beginning to hit pay dirt.

Change Your Order

You will never find your voice living from the outside in. Most of us have fallen into the trap of living backwards. The common life is defined as one that goes like this: *Have it—do it—be it.* In other words, the things you "have" define what you "do" and that "creates" who you are. This commerce-centered existence says that if you have enough of the right things—houses, jeans, Ferraris, watches, friends—and do enough of the right things—perfect job, work out, run for office, hit the sales goal—you can be what you want to be. So, how's it working for you so far?

That's what I thought.

The path to finding your voice involves reversing the order. "Being" just as you are comes first—with no strings attached—the good, the bad, and the ugly. Stand buck naked in front of a full-length mirror, and what do you see? After the initial shock, open your eyes and take a long, hard look. Good thing that's not the real *you*—it's just the machine that moves you around while you're here. So drop any thought that changing the machine changes the engine. For you wrench-heads, it's like saying that if you paint the exterior enough the engine will fix itself. You have to open the hood to get a tune-up, and your "being" will be found inside—not outside. Yeah, it takes work, but here's the cool part: once you reverse the order, the more you "be" and the less you "do," the more you'll "have." Trust me on this one.

Sing Your Song

Now that you have cleared your mind of all the "brain clutter" by writing down the things that take up most of your time and those things that give you pleasure, and you have taken the second step to change the order in which you experience life, write down this question: *What challenge in the world is in need of my voice?* Is it hunger or illiteracy or drug abuse? How about the elderly or self-esteem issues for young people or the environment? What about single parents or the homeless or adoption? Maybe it's local politics, organ donation, or alternative energy. It could be child abuse, working with the blind, or creating an after-school program where you live. The list—as with our daily challenges—is endless.

Your voice is an incredible instrument—unique unto you. The words you speak can be either saviors or swords, bridges or barriers. They can build someone up or break them down. They can inspire or inflame. They can create hope or strike fear. They can create a movement or total chaos. They can heal or break the human heart. Not everyone will agree with your voice, but that matters little. What counts is that you speak to that which moves you into greater circles of service and sheds light on the dark places. *Whatever you are seeking is seeking you.* And your voice can be the right one at just the right time that can make a difference in the way things go.

CHAPTER 3

Steady As You Go

*It's not hard to make decisions when you know
what your values are.*

—Roy Disney

On a recent trip to Florida, I was doing the usual hotel check-in routine when the clerk informed me that a small safe had been placed inside the closet of our suite, free of charge, to enable guests to keep their valuables safe while on their journey. Sure enough, when I arrived in the room, it was there. With key in hand the next morning, I was comforted by the fact that my possessions were safely locked away, and I had the only key. My valuables were safe.

So, how are your valuables these days? No, I don't mean your credit cards, jewelry, and stock certificates—those things come and go with the passing of time. I'm referring to something more sustainable—your values. Do you know what they are, and where they came from? Are they steady, or do they shift depending on the situation you are in or the people with whom you surround yourself? Do you live a value-centered life or an existence focused on a loosely constructed system that is determined by the events of the day and the weather?

Each person's value system is the foundation of his or her achievement—or lack thereof. If you watch an architect design a house, the emphasis is put on the foundation—the inner structure from which all building begins. Just as a house's foundation is crucial to its overall quality, so is our value system—our own foundation—crucial to the quality of our lives. Jim Amos is the best example I know of someone who exemplifies the principle that a strong foundation lays the groundwork for a life of service, purpose, and prosperity.

Rare is the day that James Amos Jr. does not enter my thoughts. Jim is the former President and CEO of Mail Boxes Etc. (MBE), which he helped build into a $1.5-billion business. He orchestrated the sale of MBE to United Parcel Service, which then renamed the system the UPS Store. Currently, Jim serves as Chairman Emeritus of MBE/UPS. A distinguished franchise executive, he also has served as Chairman of the International Franchise Association and more recently as Chairman of Sona MedSpa International, which was one of the companies in which Eagle Alliance Partners (his investment company) invested post-MBE. His success in franchising goes back more than 25 years, and he is widely regarded as one of the country's leading experts on the franchise industry. His business record alone qualifies him for space on these pages—and that success is a direct result of living a value-centered life.

However, it was his service in Vietnam that changed his life.

As a young Marine Corps captain, he went to the jungle with little faith and nothing more than a gung-ho attitude. Under fire and witnessing the horror and brutality of war, Jim found his faith. In that moment, the core value of faith went from an abstract idea to a concrete knowing. From a filthy foxhole emerged a new man—forged out of seeing the worst that human beings can inflict on one another—and he began to construct the values that kept his men and him alive during two combat tours in South Vietnam. He would never again have to fear what the future held because he now had a guiding set of principles by which to live. Jim received 12 decorations, including the Purple Heart and the Vietnamese Cross of Gallantry for his service and leadership. Vietnam made a lot of young men bitter, but it changed Jim Amos for the better.

Like everyone else in this book, Jim continues to contribute in as many ways as possible. He is the author of *The Memorial: A Novel of the Vietnam War* (chosen by the American Library Association as one of the best books of the year in 1990), and *The Complete Idiot's Guide to Franchising*. When I saw the reviews for *Focus or Failure*, I knew that his message not only fit my listening audience, but also was something of which all of us needed to be reminded. I felt compelled to connect with this man who had done so much, come so far, and led so many.

In the summer of 1998, we invited Jim on the show. The response from listeners was overwhelming, and for the next year we talked once a month and dissected his book from stem to stern. After doing thousands of shows, I have a pretty good idea of where a guest is coming from. I can tell the difference between those who write for the *advances they get* and those who write for the *advances they make*. At one point, I recalled one of our first conversations on the air when I decided to test Jim a little bit.

"Jim," I began, "when you talk about values in America, what seems to be the one that is most lacking?"

Jim: They are all connected. It's not like you go out one day and decide to have honesty or integrity or purpose. I don't think we are lacking certain values over others. I think most people have no idea what they value.

John: Why not?

Jim: Because we are self-absorbed—too busy, stuck in ruts we make and refuse to be responsible for. Anyone can talk about values. It's living them that matters, and in order to live them, you have to know what you stand for.

John: Why stand for anything? Why make the effort?

Jim: Because the natural human condition is one of optimism. Being pessimistic is a learned emotion. Pessimism is a result of seeing the world from the perspective of a victim—someone owes you; someone somewhere is holding you back; someone or some group is the reason you are the way you are. The only payoff in acting like a victim is the attention you get. You don't find many optimists who are not value-centered. Because they are value-centered, they know who they are. They know what they value.

Americans know right from wrong and have always risen to the occasion. But there seems to be a growing segment of society that has forgotten the basic tenets of our citizenship—personal and professional responsibility, duty to ourselves, our communities, and to our country. The greatest tragedy of our time could be the greatness we all have and let go, untested and unnoticed. Being too comfortable could be the downfall of our nation."

As he spoke, I recalled the decline of the Roman Empire and asked Jim if he ever considered a parallel between our country and the great society that no longer exists.

Jim: Edward Gibbon, who wrote *The Decline and Fall of the Roman Empire*, said that the end of Rome really came down to five factors over a period of time. First, marriages began to fail and divorce rapidly increased, which undermined the most important foundation of any society—the family. Second, taxes were pushed higher and higher over time, and the money was used not on things that sustain the society—like infrastructure—but rather on celebrations and programs that were superficial at best. Third, the insatiable need for sports by the masses and the increasing brutality of the games eroded their values. Sports had become a god. Fourth, we saw the buildup of giant armaments to keep enemies out when, in fact, the real enemy lived within its own borders—the decadence of people who had lost their vision. Finally, faith simply got lost in the shuffle. The connection to a higher power—to God—was pushed aside in favor of the gods they had created. This pursuit of wealth—all forms of pleasure at any cost, with the loss of the family unit and sports as a focal point—sounds like things we hear about on the news every day."

John: But surely we wouldn't be so ignorant as to go the way of Rome. Shouldn't we be learning lessons from the past instead of merely repeating them?

Jim: One would think so. The Roman Empire lasted around one thousand years. We have only been a country for just over two hundred and twenty years (this was in 1998), but technology has pushed the decline of our morals and values at an accelerated rate. It took Rome one thousand years to burn. We could do the job in half the time, and in so many ways it seems we are bent on creating the same fate they did.

Can you smell smoke yet?

Each of us lives by a blueprint—much of it downloaded when we were young—but more and more we are guided by things outside of ourselves. We dig ourselves into a trough of debt, and then scramble for some get-rich-quick scheme to bail us out, only to repeat the process over and over. The quest for money is the attempt to connect our values to a piece of paper with dead presidents on it. It's great to have things, but when the things have you, it becomes a problem. We are a sports-crazed society, and in many ways the highly paid, highly visible pro athlete is a god. He tells us what shoes to wear, what cell phone to use, what car to drive, and what food to eat. We connect with these larger-than-life images on a visceral level. We wish we were them because we don't know who we are. Missing the lesson and focusing on the players is a mistake. That's why we latch onto newer, younger players when others fade. They are disposable heroes.

As we build up the war machine to keep us safe in the world, our own country seems intent on exploding from within. At 8:46 A.M. on September 11, 2001, the world watched in horror as the unthinkable became a reality. In less than a couple of hours, the fabric we call America was changed forever. It was torn and tattered and burned, in some ways beyond recognition. We watched our fellow citizens leap to their deaths on television. We sat in mute disbelief as the Twin Towers fell. We cried in despair as families wandered the streets looking for loved ones. We stood silent as the news came in from the Pentagon and Pennsylvania. We mourned the loss of innocence. We also did something extraordinary—*we united*. We filled churches to overflowing. Caravans of vehicles from every corner of the map made their way to New York, laden with what was needed. Entertainers dropped their act and raised money in telethons. Schoolchildren collected spare change and held can drives. Our elected officials stood in full view together and sang with one voice. Out of chaos came order. *Why?*

Because we remembered what we had lost sight of—the things we value—home and family, loving and giving, faith and hope. We were tolerant of each other; our differences didn't matter anymore. America was united once again in a common cause and with a common bond—tragedy. We hoisted the flag, gave speeches, and vowed to rebuild, respond, and reclaim our greatness.

It lasted about six months—maybe.

In just five years, it's a different world. The gap between the right and the left makes the Grand Canyon look like a sand trap and leaves those in the middle shaking their heads. Governmental and corporate corruption is rampant, and our sports gods are not getting paid enough to play a game while schools are struggling to keep their doors open. We have once again become like so many cows in the field, chewing cud, beating our gums about how the guy across the street is wrong and how we are right. We are told day and night that the terrorists could strike at any time, and we live in a state of fear that is bound by duct tape and color-coded alerts that no one pays attention to anymore.

September 11th was a stark reminder of what each of us holds dear—what we value—but it has since eroded into a political and philosophical debate that will only serve to put into motion one of the most important laws of the universe: *Lessons are repeated until they are learned.*

In an office lined with books and medals, James Amos, Jr. is bringing his very core to the business world, and common sense suggests that the most simple of answers are usually the ones that have the most profound impact on our lives. Holding the line on personal values is the antidote to the erosion of society we see around us. Jim has leaned on certain values that have always come through for him without fail. Faith, family, and fortune are all part of his world because he took the time to determine what he values most. I have a lot of hope because Jim is in the thick of things. For every Enron scandal, there is someone like Jim leading in the opposite direction. It's not the system that's the problem; it's the people within the system who end up in the headlines. Trying to do anything—running a business, creating a better relationship, being a more effective parent, or starting over after buildings are blown apart—is like being the captain of a rudderless ship without a congruent set of values. You get to see a lot of the ocean, but rarely find your destination. And even if you do, you might not know it, for how can you recognize that which has no value to you?

With the push and pull of a country that is still trying to define itself, the possibility of slipping into the abyss of moral decay is ever present. The slide to a legacy like that of Rome looms larger every day. It is a path to mental, physical, and spiritual destruction we seem to be bent on living. One hundred and forty-three years ago, America fought a civil war with cannons and bayonets. All these years later, we fight the "uncivil war" with words on talk radio and morning news shows. With the ongoing push and pull of the media infusing our minds with how "they" think we should be, now is the time to define what is near and dear to us as never before.

The values that Jim Amos instills in his companies and his life are nothing new, but unlike most people, he doesn't just talk about them—he lives them. He believes in these values: caring for our neighbors and ourselves; being *honest*, not just some of the time, but all of the time, no matter the consequence; *fairness* in our dealings with others, both personally and professionally; *integrity* in all that we do so that there is no temptation to become divided within; building a sense of trust with the people in our lives; *respect* for ourselves so we can then receive it from others; commitment to an ideal or goal that challenges us; *accountability* for the things we do and don't do. These values got generations of people before us through the Depression, World War II, Korea, Vietnam, recessions, and some pretty difficult times, and they can be the stone and mortar by which we build our own lives. These are challenging times—and maybe that's the point. Without struggle, there is little growth. Without growth, there is no change. And if things don't change, the more they stay the same—*unless we change them*. Pretty simple, isn't it?

Of course, there is Option B: you can simply turn on the TV and watch the world slowly devour itself without lifting a finger, thinking that whatever comes down the pipe is just fine and one person doesn't make a difference. It's all a choice. An old African proverb states, "If there is no enemy within, the enemies outside can do no harm." What you value most in your life is what you will see increase in your life. So how are your investments paying off these days?

We live in a time of more change, more excess, and more fear than at any other time in American history. But there is at the core of every American a deep sense of value, of what is good and true. When we operate from that place of conviction, we can literally change the course of history. And in our struggles, the one card to call on is our values.

—James Amos Jr.

Protect Your Valuables

Imagine you are at the helm of a very important company. Every day and in every way, your attention is needed on make-or-break decisions. People are constantly calling upon your leadership skills, abilities, and resources. You are an expert at "multitasking" and making sure that all the bases are covered when it comes to business, and you intimately know everyone from the receptionist to the top salesperson to the managers and janitors. After years in the business, you still understand that you don't know it all and that at any moment it could all change. At the end of the day, behind the closed door with the sign that says "Chief Executive Officer," you put up your feet and count your blessings, realizing how much value your position and presence brings to so many people.

The reality is that each of us owns and operates a very important business—*our business*. While the above scenario might describe one of Jim's days, it also could be the kind of schedule a parent or entrepreneur or teacher would keep. CEO in this case would stand for Confidence Equals Outcome. This type of equation is made possible because of the values that Jim has identified and exemplifies. He will not budge from them for any amount of fame or fortune—and because of that stance, he has plenty of both. He is confident that the values he has woven into his personal and professional life will always work—because they always have. You might never put together a massive merger or be a consultant to industry, but you are the Chairperson of the Board of your life—the salesperson, janitor, secretary, marketing department, and management all in one. How would your business grow if all those parts were in line with your values?

The values by which Jim Amos lives are not exclusive to him. They are readily available to you. Once you define *and* refine them, you can count on them. Here are five value options with which you should consider adopting or getting re-acquainted.

Dare to Care

When I was growing up in the late '60s and early '70s, the rally cry of a generation was "change the world for the better." It seems today's generation is more interested in "owning the world forever." They have seen millions of dollars made by rappers, rock stars, and reality contestants. Ask a teenager today what he or she would like to do, and you will likely hear being on *American Idol* or inventing video games as the most frequent answer. Neither of those in and of itself is bad, but without the component of caring, all success is empty. Every disaster showcases the caring we have as a nation. It's of utmost importance to make sure that caring is not just used for the big picture. Extend yourself in the small, nameless ways. It's been proven time and time again that caring about those around us always comes back to us. At some point in our lives, we extend our hand—to pull someone up or to allow someone to lift us up. When you care about yourself, the natural tendency is to care for others as well. And you can never care enough because it always pays off . . . *all-ways*.

Honesty Is the *Only* Policy

Webster's defines honesty as "fairness and straightforward conduct and an uprightness of character." Our world is filled with images that mock the value of honesty: lobbyists and politicians on the take, raking in millions until either they get caught or their conscience begins to eat them up from the inside out. The media especially is a haven for "reality" shows that pit one contestant against another, and in order to "win" they often resort to lying, cheating, and backstabbing. With money as the usual prize, how do you convey to people that honesty is one value that is worth hanging on to? Actually, the answer is pretty simple: look at the results. "What goes around comes around," and no one ever really gets away with anything. The reality-show winner who forgoes paying his taxes ends up doing time. The athlete who shaves points and won't admit it gets barred for life. The politician who doles out contracts to his or her buddies comes crashing down in a news conference. I am convinced that many people feel that they are justified not telling the truth or acting in ways that are not in line with being honest feel they are justified because "everyone else does it." That's the point: *don't be like everyone else.* Be a better you. Set a new standard, raise the bar—just for you. If someone else latches on, that's great. If not, at least you will know that when your head hits the pillow at night, your honesty is intact. It's a feeling that's not easy to come by when you are lying in bed wondering if you covered your tracks or in a prison cot thinking that, in hindsight, being honest might have been a better way to go.

Integrity Is an Inside Job

Integrity is another word that's often bantered about but not well-defined. So here's the official definition: *Integrity is the incorruptible core of humanity.* While that sounds lofty, I must remind you of two things. First, we all have a corruptible core. Second, the core you choose to focus on is the one you get to spend time with. My Native American friends tell the story of a young man who comes to the lodge and speaks with his great-grandfather. "I had a vision last night. There were two wolves inside me, fighting for my attention. They were both starving and wanted to be fed. What does this mean?" The elder carefully said, "Inside each of us lives two wolves. One is a black wolf that is filled with jealousy, rage, hatred, and judgment. His anger and pain have rendered him nearly blind to anything but his own existence. The other wolf is white and is filled with hope, peace, love, tolerance, and understanding. His pain has connected him to the whole of humanity that he resides in, but is often forgotten. Both feed off the human spirit for their nourishment." The young man paused and said, "Which one will survive?" The elder simply said, "The one you feed the most." Integrity is not just about how you act; *it's also about who you are.*

Trust Is a Must

Just about every corner of our society has a component of trust; conversely, a large number of people claim to have "trust issues." Maybe if we looked at a few places where we have to trust ourselves and others (and may not even know it), we could see trust in a different light. For instance, when you are driving, the only thing that keeps traffic apart is a line of yellow paint—and we trust that everyone else on the road took the same driver's education course as we did! If you have ever visited a pharmacy, you are trusting that the pharmacist knows what he or she is doing. Same goes for doctors, dentists, and therapists. Ever had your vehicle repaired? How about when you put your money in the bank? When you send your kids to school, you have to trust the system to educate them. The post office is nothing more than trust in motion. The list of opportunities for us to trust on a daily basis is almost endless, but it's a two-way street. Be someone whom others can trust. The payoff will be enormous.

"Faith" Your Fears

Most of us go through life afraid—and with good reason. We are shown images every single day that validate our suspicion that the world is a place to be feared. Consumers get ripped off; major corporations collapse; politicians are on the take; mass murderers get out of prison on a technicality; sharks attack off the coast; airplanes collide in mid-air; people are poisoned by tainted meat, toxic water, and polluted air—and that's just the first five minutes of the late news! We have programmed ourselves into a constant state of fear, which contributes very little to living an uncommon life.

Faith is the only antidote that I know of for "fear overdose." Faith has many definitions: belief in a force greater than oneself, fidelity to one's promises, and a strong belief or conviction. I am partial to St.Augustine's view of faith: *to believe what you do not see.* The reward of this faith is to see what you believe. In order to fear something, you have to believe in it. The same goes for faith. Essentially, you bring forth that on which you focus. If what we focus on expands, *then it is possible that fear is nothing more than the opportunity to display faith.* They are two sides of the same coin.

I suggest you take a moment to define faith for yourself—what it means, how you display it, and what role it plays in your life. There are as many definitions for faith as there are people, and it's essential that you identify it. Once you do, make a short list of all the times that faith, *as you define it,* made a difference in your life. Faith and fear both create results: one can move you forward; the other can hold you back. In which direction have you been moving lately?

CHAPTER 4

It Begins and Ends with You

The willingness to accept responsibility for one's own life is the source from which self-respect springs.

—Joan Didion

When I first started in radio, I truly had no idea if anyone would listen, or buy advertising on the show, or grasp the concept of a show that catered to the masses, not the minority. What that means to me is that the subjects and issues I lean toward affect all of us in some way, shape, or form, from parenting to business and personal success to handling the adversity that life throws our way roughly every 90 days or so—no matter how you vote. It's easy to get on radio and wait for the morning headlines, open up the phone lines, and ask people to weigh in on something they have no control over. The radio airwaves are filled with rhetoric and opinion, and so much of it is a lower vibration. Every murder is dissected in public. Every celebrity screw-up is probed in depth. We have been trained like Pavlov's dogs to respond to the "if it bleeds, it leads" stories that are really none of our business. A steady diet of murder, arson, rape, death, and who-is-doing-what-to-the-neighbor's-cat stories only reinforces the media-induced perception that the world is a scary place and you could be its next lead story. I am convinced that this influx of negative news has given birth to the "I'm not responsible" mentality that permeates so much of our 21st-century world. We are all waiting to be the next victim, so why not act like one?

Years ago at a Windstar Symposium, Chief Oren Lyons of the Onondaga Tribe referred to responsibility as *the ability to respond,* and his observation has never left my mind. Being a person of *responsibility* is to be someone who has learned the ability to respond to whatever life presents. But when the subject of responsibility comes up, most of us turn away. We have all heard the word, but we take the power it contains for granted. The very moment that you let go of all that look-what-they-did-to-me stuff is the moment you claim victory over your lower self. When I think of the more than 5,000 guests who have spent time with me over the years, one name keeps rising to the top in terms of personal responsibility—*the ability to respond*—and that's Cheryl Richardson.

In some respects, doing thousands of shows with a slant on empowerment can get old fast. This is radio we are talking about—"theater of the mind"—and one has to have the ability to entertain while informing and inspiring at the same time. Energy created between the host and guest is akin to lighting fireworks when it's raining—if you've got a wet wick, no fireworks. One of the things that stand out in my mind with regard to Cheryl is her deep commitment to a cause. The burning desire to inform people of what she has learned shines through on every single show we have done together. Cheryl is a skyrocket waiting for launch on *and* off the air.

Cheryl was the first President of the International Coach Federation and holds one of their first Master Certified Coach credentials. She is also the recipient of the 2000 Motivational Book Award for *Life Makeovers* from Books for a Better Life, which honors the year's most outstanding books and magazines in the self-improvement genre.

Cheryl was the team leader for the Lifestyle Makeover Series on "The Oprah Winfrey Show," and she accompanied Oprah on the "Live Your Best Life" nationwide tour. Cheryl served as the co-executive producer and host of "The Life Makeover Project with Cheryl Richardson" on the Oxygen Network and as the co-executive producer and host of two public television specials—"Stand Up for Your Life" and "Create an Abundant Life."

The woman is *serious* about her business.

Cheryl made her first appearance on my show right after her book, *Take Time for Your Life*, was released. In our first conversation, I noticed that there was a real edge to the material she was presenting. Cheryl put out this book with a clear intent: personal responsibility is the key to personal freedom. It was not too long after that show that Oprah Winfrey showcased Cheryl's work to the world. The best thing about her success is that after years of hard work with small groups of people and in one-on-one situations, Cheryl Richardson became a role model for people to understand how important it is to carve out time for the best within so that each life reflects a greater truth.

As Cheryl's star rose, her demand by the media did as well, but she always made time to do radio with me—and thousands of people listening in on our conversations. A few months after September 11, we spoke about the events of that day. There was a real urgency in her message that hit the nail on the head in terms of what is and is not important in life—and it happened in the first 60 seconds of discussing her latest book.

John: What is the overriding message of "Stand Up for Your Life"?

Cheryl: To stay awake.

John: What does that mean?

Cheryl: On September 11, 2001, a dramatic shift happened in the consciousness of America. We watched in horror as people leapt from buildings to their death. The Towers fell to the Earth and changed the landscape forever. We were challenged to never return to the lives we all knew. It was a cataclysmic event in more ways than one.

John: How so?

Cheryl: I believe in those hours, days, and weeks following, we were fully awake for the first time in decades. Our focus shifted from all the little distractions of life to the things that are important. We gave blood, money, time, and prayers. Churches were full, and "one nation indivisible" meant something. People who were in the process of getting divorces reconsidered; families that were ending had new beginnings. We hugged our children closer and said, "I love you" with meaning. The fabric of life had changed.

John: So how are we doing now?

Cheryl: I fear we're going back to sleep. My crusade, if you will, is to make sure we don't fall asleep, that we remember the things we connected with after this horrifying wake-up call. Standing up for your life is not an option; it's a necessity.

Again, that was the first minute of the show, and it escalated from there.

John: Cheryl, there seems to be a really strange trait that humanity has: we are a forgetful species. I'm not talking about misplacing the car keys or buying cat litter at the store. We vow "Never again!" and then we do. We say we will learn from the past, and we repeat it. We declare that this time things will be different, and we go back to doing the same thing over and over again—and expecting our lives to change. You would think that with all the technological advances we have made somehow a human's ability to clearly see that the circumstances they have created give birth to the results they experience would be obvious.

Cheryl: John, I don't really know what it takes for people to learn. It seems that it always comes down to pain or pleasure—the carrot and the stick. Some of us chase the carrot, and others need to be whacked by the stick from which it was hanging. Life is difficult enough without adding to the chaos by shifting our responsibility to others. The moment you think, "I'm not responsible for this mess," is the moment you can make the decision to help clean it up, regardless of your prior participation. Humans are the only species that has the ability to make decisions based on memory that can improve the outcome. Every other creature runs on instinct. The fact is that I have never coached anyone who did not have the ability to make the changes they were seeking. They simply could not see the blind spots that held them back or the stepping-stones to their dreams. That's what a coach does— helps the player see what he cannot. But a coach can't play the game, and to me life is the most important game there is. It's my mission to inspire people who are ready and willing—because *we are all able*—to make positive changes in our lives and the world.

I mentioned earlier in this book that I had the chance to donate a kidney to my daughter Amanda. One of the results of that decision was that after taking nine weeks off the air and returning to a national audience—a goal that took years to achieve—I knew that I really needed more time off. The challenge of running the business—finding and maintaining advertisers, writing the Powerthoughts vignettes, not to mention airing a three-hour-a-day show, five days a week—on top of donating one of my organs really took its toll. I had nothing left in my tank. It was one of the most difficult decisions I ever had to make in my life. I had a family to take care of, not to mention a pile of medical bills. I had investors who had funded the day-to-day operations. I had thousands of people who were used to turning on the radio and hearing my voice, as well as guests who had found a home for their message. Agonizingly, I pulled the plug on New Year's Eve 2002. I was relieved and depressed at the same time, and I didn't know if I would ever return to radio. I was totally responsible for the decision and outcome, no matter what it might be.

In the nearly three years I was off the radio, I spent much of that time working on this book, but not a day went by that I didn't think I somehow made a mistake or screwed up. One day, I happened to be walking through a bookstore, and sitting on a shelf in the new-release section was *The Unmistakable Touch of Grace* by Cheryl Richardson. It was like a billboard to me from the Almighty. This happened at one of the lowest points in my self-imposed hiatus, and I knew it was no coincidence. My next phone call was to Jan Silva, one of Cheryl's assistants, who was really happy to hear from me. A couple of days later, my phone rang, and the voice on the other end had a hard-to-miss Boston accent. "Hey, John, it's Cheryl!"

We started out talking about her book, and then, in true coach form, she put it right on my back with regard to my decision to leave radio and see what else the universe might have in store. When we finished, I felt like I had gone ten rounds with Rocky Balboa—mentally. Our conversation helped to remind me of who I was and what I was capable of, what I had already accomplished and, more importantly, what I was responsible for during my watch. A few months later, Cheryl and I spoke again at length, which served to ignite the flame even more. The woman is a very tough taskmaster when it comes to achieving goals and being responsible for the outcome. She cuts no slack before its time.

Every Sunday evening in my e-mail box is a newsletter from Cheryl, and each month it includes a notice about a monthly telegathering—a giant conference call open to members on her online community. One topic in particular caught my eye: using mistakes as opportunities to change. I had never called in on a teleconference for anything, but I felt compelled to listen in, so I called at the appropriate time and listened to people who obviously knew each other (at least over the phone). Shortly, there was that unmistakable Massachusetts lilt welcoming the listeners. Cheryl asked the callers to all say, "good evening," and one by one they did, so I did as well. Then Cheryl said, "Hold on a second. John, is that you?" So much for remaining anonymous on a coaching call!

Cheryl so graciously introduced me to the throng of listeners as "the most influential talk-radio host on the dial," and in short order her loyal listeners were chiming in about how they hoped they could hear my show where they lived. One woman declared, "It sounds like John is a change agent." Their words spurred me on, and it was the final step in making my way back to the microphone. Thanks to all of you—wherever you are.

After 33 months, I returned to radio, and, of course, there could only be one choice for my first guest: Cheryl Richardson. In many ways, it was like I had never gone off the air, but I knew in many other ways that the hiatus had served as a time of self-reflection and self-determination, and I took the opportunity to let listeners know how much Cheryl's coaching and friendship played a part in my return. True to form, she thanked me, and then proceeded to verbally construct a blueprint for people who are seeking to build a life that is founded on being personally responsible for all the steps they take.

We spoke at length about *The Unmistakable Touch of Grace* (a very powerful book about her journey), and I was so impressed with her brutally honest look at her own life. Many "self-help" authors just recycle old material. Cheryl's work is born from experience. One story in particular marks the point where she decided to take responsibility for her own life.

As a young woman, Cheryl admitted to living a pretty unconscious life doing the 9-to-5 grind and spending weekends partying with friends. One weekend while at a bar with co-workers, she had a strange experience that brought her a sense of clarity. She heard a voice say, "Cheryl, you don't belong here. You're meant to do so much more with your life."

In that one moment, the little voice we all have—but mostly

ignore—changed her life. Grace had intervened, and the result was total responsibility for her existence—no matter what—from then on. And because of Cheryl's willingness to share her path—with all its highs and lows and accounts of divine interventions—she somehow was granting others permission to do the same. Her work in the world is very important, but none of it would exist if she had not taken total responsibility for who she was—and who she could become.

Responsibility—the ability to respond—is quite possibly the most powerful tool you have for making positive, lasting change in your life. And the most amazing thing is that the moment you declare "I'm responsible," old doors close and new ones open, as they did for Cheryl. The word *victor* replaces *victim*, and so many of the dreams you have forgotten come true. Pretty good deal, huh?

Developing your inner life should be your first priority. It's all about waking up and becoming conscious of who you are and not hiding your power anymore. It's about being fully responsible for becoming all you are capable of being.

—Cheryl Richardson

The Responsibility Factor

I am not sure when or where we got disconnected from responsibility. "It's not my job, man" has become a popular cultural phrase. Well, it must be someone's job somewhere. Humans are paradoxical creatures: we want life to be different, and yet so often we are unwilling to take any responsibility to change the very things that hold us back. We have been conditioned to think someone else will take care of it, or life will just magically get better if we file our taxes on time or get organized at the office. I am amazed at the very thin line we each walk every day, not knowing if we will be here in the next moment or ten years down the line. It makes perfect common sense to me that responsibility for our actions and a responsibility to this little blue ball that hangs in space without our permission should be given higher priority than what we have previously given them.

This book is all about common sense, so get this one right out of the gate: *you are totally responsible for your thoughts, actions, and words, no matter what*—period, end of story. The moment you shift from "look what I did" to "look what they did to me"—or even worse, "look what you *made* me do"—you have lost all your power to influence or change any aspect of your life.

Our individual ability to respond is what change and evolution are all about. If you don't respond to changing climates and conditions, you will end up in a museum stuffed with your own attitudes toward this precious gift called life. And by the way, we are always on the clock—and you are running out of time every single second.

The next time you feel like playing "Blame Them Poker," remember that the responsibility card beats the victim card every round.

Slice the Cheese

My grandfather came to America from Sweden and brought with him the time-honored tradition of eating limpa bread (a light, seedless rye) and cheese. I couldn't have been much more than five or six when he put me on his knee and cut me a slice of bread with cheese. Of course, the real treat was sitting with Grandpa Carl. He would say, "No matter how thin you cut the cheese, there are always two sides." When it comes to being responsible in your life, you can only control your side of the cheese, but the opportunity exists to be 100 percent responsible for your 50 percent. Be vigilant about not insisting that others be responsible for their part. Either they will or they won't, but that is out of your control. It might be a good idea to keep a piece of cheese in your purse or wallet for those times when you feel the "victim thing" coming on. Let it serve as a reminder that if you claim responsibility for your half, that's as good as it gets.

Note of caution: If you choose this exercise, make sure it's not Gouda cheese, and it's wrapped in cellophane.

Bite Your Tongue

The next time you feel the need to start blaming someone else for whatever circumstances you might be experiencing, give your *median fibrous septum* (that divider that runs down the center of your tongue) a nice, firm clamp. After you do that a few times, you will actually be programming your brain to stop thinking like a victim. It's the same thing as repeatedly hitting yourself in the head with a hammer until you realize that it hurts—and you stop. No matter how strong the urge is to fire up the "blamethrower," hold your tongue until the urge passes. You will be amazed at how quickly "look what happened to me" leaves your vocabulary.

It's Not Their Fault—Really

There are six billion humans on the Earth, and each of us carries a belief system that is reinforced by how we choose to see the world. Politics, economics, ethics, religion, and a myriad of information shape our beliefs. Being "right" keeps the belief system intact, no matter how "wrong" those beliefs might be to others. The only way you can maintain a victim stance is by not seeing the other side of things. If you can put yourself in someone else's life, you might be very surprised at how much they feel like a victim, too. This does not mean you condone or accept their behavior, but it does mean you make an attempt to understand their points of reference. When you do, the gap closes, and you are less likely to walk around saying, "So-and-so is the reason I am who I am," because chances are pretty good they are saying the same thing about you. So, who is right? I could give you the answer, but searching it out for yourself might be a better idea.

Take on More Responsibility

While most of us shy away from responsibility, consider that *what you focus on the longest becomes the strongest.* So, the less you want responsibility, the more you will get because you are so focused on it. When you embrace responsibility, it becomes an opportunity and not a burden. Face it head-on. Volunteer in your community, run for office, raise your hand in class, and put yourself in situations that are connected to you being responsible for an outcome. By standing in the light of responsibility, the shadows that most people associate with it—failure or blame—simply fade away. Every person featured in this book eventually sat down one day and had this talk with themselves: "OK, it's time to be responsible for my life, no matter what." That's why they succeed. Few ever blame their way to fame—and if they do, it doesn't last very long.

Learn Response-*Ability*

Most of us feel that responsibility is a heavy burden, when in fact the opposite is true. The more responsible you become, the less of a load you have to carry. Responsibility proves that results speak for themselves. Most of us have no idea what our responsibility reserves can do—because we shy away from anything that smacks of being responsible. Here is a surefire way to see responsibility as a blessing and not a burden. For one day, be responsible for the results you create. Be honest, trusting, and caring, and stand upright with integrity. The simple statement *"I'm responsible"*—whether the outcome is positive or negative—will set you free. If you are still blaming someone else for your life and you are older than, say, a third-grader, it's time to do some major internal excavation—or just continue the course you are on. My suggestion? Put a nice hunk of Limburger on your tongue and bite down. If you really want to blame someone for the way your life is, buy a mirror. You might not be responsible for the event that allowed you to be a victim, but you are totally in control of your response-*ability* to that event. Let it go and get on with your life.

CHAPTER 5

Truth or Consequences

Truth does not cease to exist just because it is being ignored.

—John St.Augustine

I f ever there were a "can-of-worms chapter" in this book, here it is. The subject of truth—who defines it, who decides it, and who is telling it—leaves gaps equal in size to the circumference of our planet. You might recall the famous game show of the '60s called *To Tell the Truth* where contestants pretended to be someone other than who they were, and a panel had to decide who was telling the truth.

Sounds like the Sunday morning political shows. Sounds like pro sports. Sounds like most of what comes to our ears on a daily basis. After sitting behind a microphone for thousands of shows, I have come to the following conclusion: all of us are telling our version of the truth—the one we are most comfortable with, the one that will challenge us the least, and the one that we make fit into our beliefs. While the truth might be incontrovertible, it is also open to interpretation—at least we think so—and so it is.

There are more levels to truth than a 50-story parking garage. There is truth that carries major religious overtones, truth that carries major scientific overtones, truth that carries major political overtones, truth that carries major judicial overtones. There is truth that is about personal conduct, truth connected to moral conduct, truth with regard to academic conduct, truth that underscores spiritual conduct—and the list goes on and on.

I happened to catch an old rerun of *Perry Mason* (another '60s flashback) the other day. In glorious black-and-white (which makes gray when mixed), the witness took the stand, placed her hand on the Bible, and heard the bailiff say those famous words: "Do you swear to tell the truth, the whole truth, and nothing but the truth, so help you God?"

Maybe it should be rewritten this way: "Do you swear to tell your version of the truth and at least the portion of the truth you believe in most?" You see, that's what humans do. We live our version of the truth based on the beliefs we hold. In essence, no one ever lies—all of us are right, about everything, all the time. Here are a few famous examples: "I did not have sex with that woman." "Read my lips—no new taxes!" "The gloves don't fit!" "I never had plastic surgery." "We needed that $6,000 shower curtain." "I have never taken steroids." "Everything in the book is based on events that I thought were real."

Religious doctrine or law books or a polygraph machine do not determine the line between what is real—and what is not. It is drawn by each of us based on what we think passes for truth. Humans are the only creatures who have the ability to change the course and direction of their existence, and yet most do not. They believe that a better life— more happiness, increased health or wealth, a life filled with purpose— is available to "other people." Nothing could be further from the truth.

It is very easy to add up all the bad or negative things that have been put upon our backs as humans. You can validate the pain in life by simply turning on the television or reading the headlines. It's easy to believe that what we see on the news is the truth of what is going on in the world, and you would have evidence to back it up. But there is also evidence to suggest that a far greater truth exists, and it shows up only when we allow it. No one I have ever spent time with represents that truth more than Dr. Wayne Dyer.

Wayne would have plenty of reasons to not live at the highest level possible. Moved around from orphanages to foster homes, Wayne has authored more than 15 bestsellers, including *Your Erroneous Zones*, *Pulling Your Own Strings*, and my personal favorites, *Real Magic* and *Wisdom of the Ages*. He has appeared on thousands of television shows and is hailed as the father of motivation by his legions of readers. He is also relentless in his search for truth.

I remember the very first show we did together. Wayne talked about a time when he was a young man watching *The Tonight Show* and proclaimed that he would one day be a guest on the late-night fixture. Years later, that dream came true. His point was that the universe has no time frame—only humans do—and that thoughts, either "good" or "bad," have no expiration date. That would explain the endless circles most of us dance in day after day.

I am like a kid waiting in line at the movies whenever Wayne is on the guest list. Maybe it's because spending an hour with him reminds me of the built-in truth that most of us hide or allow to rust over. We are more than our circumstances, but we are bound or free as our thoughts dictate. He is sometimes abruptly honest in his words. More than one time have I caught myself wondering, *If this type of thought process works for Wayne Dyer, a regular guy by all observations, why do two out of three people watch* Wheel of Fortune *every night instead of creating their own?*

A snippet of conversation on air with Wayne sounds like this:

John: So, what's new in the world?

Wayne: John, did you ever have the thought that the world only exists on a day-to-day basis because of the thoughts people have?

John: Run that by me again.

Wayne: Since everything is energy at the most cellular level, the creation of our surroundings comes from how we imagine the world to be. It is nothing more and nothing less than a reflection of how we think.

John: And . . .

Wayne: The poverty, war, famine, abuse, despair, and depression in the world in and of themselves mean nothing. We could easily wake up tomorrow and create the total opposite of what we are experiencing.

John: Then why don't we?

Wayne: Too busy fighting over who is right and watching television.

It has been said that the truth hurts, but it will also set you free. Seekers spend precious hours digging in themselves for that moment when they are released from yesterday's lie and are firmly established in the truth of what is possible for one person to accomplish. They know the truth that all of their needs are fulfilled and to want anything is contrary to natural law. Desire has far more power and meaning to it than most of us realize. When Wayne Dyer gets up on stage or walks the beach looking for the early morning rays of sunlight—or even does the show from his cell phone while he is jogging for this 30th year in a row—I remember that truth, much like opinion, is open for debate. But debating will not change the fact that there is one man who made a choice to use his life as an example of the ultimate truth. Our word is law, our actions create a ripple effect, and if one person creates a life based on inspiration—not desperation—then what holds the rest of us back?

One conversation I had with Wayne sticks out more than any other. Just a day after 9/11, we received a call from Wayne's publicist informing us that Wayne was grounded in a motel and wanted to talk about his book, *There's a Spiritual Solution to Every Problem*, which coincidentally came out on September 11, 2001. If ever there was a day that people needed to hear his message—and if ever there was a problem that needed to be viewed from a spiritual perspective—it was the events of 9/11.

So Wayne and I talked. "Wayne, we are experiencing a time unlike any other with the attacks on New York, Washington, and Pennsylvania. What lessons are we supposed to learn, if any, from this, and how do we as a people respond to this kind of hate against our country?"

"John, while it seems that this time is unlike any other, just 60 years ago Pearl Harbor was bombed. That, of course, was a military target, but the loss of life was staggering—and on our shores, which had never happened before. The basis of all hatred is the lie of separation—that we are a threat to each other because we are different. At various times, we have been conditioned to hate Germans, Japanese, North Koreans, the British, and others. They have been conditioned to do the same back to us. Then there is the lie of righteousness—that God somehow thinks war is a good idea, and that the all-knowing, all-creating principle that runs the universe is on one side, but not the other. So this is a challenging time for all people. We are more capable than ever before of making sure the human species becomes extinct at the push of a button. We have been killing each other for a long time, and when a majority of people begin to see the truth—that we are one creation, like a tree with many branches, and that what we do to another we do to ourselves—perhaps then we will have real peace."

"So are you saying that it's better to fight fire with water? Are you suggesting that we simply turn the other cheek?"

"I am saying that the people who inflicted this carnage should be held responsible, and that each of us are, as you say, better firefighters with water than flamethrowers."

Five years have passed since that conversation, but I listen to the tape often to remind myself that each day behind the microphone I have a choice to fan the flames in the world or offer a few buckets of water. And so do you.

If we do not start living out of the truth—that we are powerful beyond measure; that if we can inflict massive pain in the world, then we are capable of creating massive healing as well; that if we are capable of destroying each other and ourselves, then we are just as capable of supporting each other and ourselves—then we have to live with the consequences of the lies or the opposite of truth. Both truth and non-truth are based on cause and effect.

It all comes down to your ability to discern beliefs from knowing. Wayne often speaks of the difference. "Beliefs are handed down generation to generation. Beliefs are not often challenged, but merely accepted. We believe in what we do because someone conditioned us to think, act, and speak a certain way. Our view of the world as either a fearful place or an incredible opportunity is shaped by beliefs. The problem with beliefs is that when you need one, and it doesn't turn out the way you believed it would, you have nothing to fall back on. Let's say that you have a deep belief that God will protect you and your family, and then you find yourself in an auto accident that claims the life of a loved one. Most people then spend the rest of their lives blaming the God they had previously believed in. Knowing is a far more powerful state of being. It is born out of experience, not just thought. If you know that God has a plan for our lives and someone is lost in a car accident, it would be no less painful or devastating, but knowing would lead to your healing, not your undoing. Transcending beliefs into knowing is essential for living life at a higher level of awareness."

Humans are sometimes a little slow on the uptake. As a society, we will spend more on entertainment than education, and our spiritual growth has not kept up with all the technological advances we have made. There is a profound imbalance in our part of the world. In the most powerful nation on Earth, more people vote for a singer on television than for a president. We are still fighting wars started generations ago, and for the most part there is still a "you or me" rather than a "you and me" attitude in the world. That mindset didn't work 500 years ago, and it hasn't gotten much better. Wayne Dyer has been exhorting us for years to reach within as to not go without. He insists that everything we see is an illusion created by a lifetime of conditioning based on someone else's view of what is possible, what the world should be and who we are. Over 30 years have passed since I first heard a Wayne Dyer tape, and I will never forget the opening statement on the first one: "The minute you think you know everything there is to know is the moment you need to begin again." It's hard to tell the truth when no one wants to listen, but perhaps "if it hurts, it instructs" will someday teach us that in the end, like it or not, we are really all the same.

Imagine for a moment if everything you believed to be true wasn't. What would you do? Who would you be? What truth would you seek? Where would you start?

In Wayne Dyer's world, he has come to know that what is true for one is true for all. If we would just put down the clicker, imagine the world that waits.

You have as much right to live your highest truth as Einstein, Galileo, and Gandhi. You have access to the same Source they did. Change the way you look at things, and the things you look at change.

—Wayne Dyer

Be True to Yourself

An old story goes something like this. A young couple gets married. The new bride offers to cook dinner for her husband's entire family on Easter. She spends a full night and day getting ready for the feast. As the whole family is seated around the table, she enters the room with a beautifully prepared ham. The guests recoil in horror because the young bride didn't cut off the ends of the ham—a family tradition! She drops the dish and runs into the kitchen, sobbing at her ineptness. Her husband dares to ask out loud, *"Why do we cut off the ends of the ham every Easter?"* They look at each other without an answer, until the great-grandmother speaks up. "My mother would cut off the ends of the ham because otherwise it wouldn't fit in the pan."

I submit to you that many of us are cutting off the ends of our ham and have no clue why. Getting to the truth of why we do what we do, live the way we live, think the way we think, and believe what we believe should be a top priority. The "penalty" for doing what you have always done is a life filled with confusion, victimization, and lack. The "reward" for digging through your belief systems—testing each belief to see if it's yours or passed on by your parents, a neighbor, or some talk radio host—is a life filled with clarity, contentment and abundance. There is not one area of our lives that is not affected by our beliefs in one way, shape, or form. You can either live the truth or live the consequences, but you cannot live both at the same time.

Once again, someone (Wayne Dyer) has overcome difficult circumstances (living in foster homes and orphanages and an alcoholic father) to create a life of success (best-selling author, sought-after speaker, and world-class father) because he connected with the highest truth. And the only time it costs you anything is when you don't use it.

Make a List

Here we go again. I cannot stress enough how important is the exercise of writing. Our mind, incredible as it may be, is also like a large dumpster. It catches and holds everything that has ever been said to us, and we regurgitate information without even knowing where it comes from. Write down everything you believe is true in the left margin of the paper, and I mean everything—your beliefs on food, sex, marriage, work, religion, exercise, politics, education, community, ethnicity, money, you name it. After you complete the list, start a middle column and write a short sentence about why you believe each of these things. Once done, go to the right margin and name the person or place you learned the belief. Take your time: internal excavation cannot be rushed. When you are done, you have just cleared your mind cache of its most important cargo—your beliefs—and they are no longer hidden in the recesses of your mind. They are in the light of day on plain paper.

Pick Five

From the list you have created, pick five beliefs. These are the ones you are going to test. Let's use a belief about money, for example. While the Treasury burns more in one day than most people earn in a lifetime, most people believe there is not enough to go around. For one day, observe how you think about money, how you treat money, how you talk about money, how you spend your money. Just make a few mental notes about the truth you assign to a piece of green paper with a dead president on it. On day two, observe how other people treat, talk about, and spend their money. Now here is the kicker: call your local banker and ask him if he thinks there is enough money in the world. Or you can just guess his or her answer. We get what we think is true for us—nothing more, nothing less. Go through the beliefs that you wrote down. Are they building you up? Or holding you back?

Build a Lie Detector

This one is easy, and you don't have to be CSI-certified to do it. Once you have your list of beliefs, notice when you use them. Every time you make a false statement you think is true, like "Money doesn't grow on trees," pull on your right ear really hard and make some electrical-type noise, like "Z-Z-Z-Z-Z." First and foremost, you will look really stupid doing this in public. Second, if you are going to be conditioned by society, you might as well get in on it yourself. Last, you will see in short order how many non-truths you have been living. And money does, in fact, grow on trees.

The Truth Is Ever Expanding

Living in a world of non-truth (limiting beliefs) is a surefire way to stay small, controlled, and fearful. Stepping into the world of truth (solid, concrete knowing) is an ever-expanding adventure. As Wayne so often says, "*When you change the way you look at things, the things you look at change.*" It's more than just a catchy mantra. It's real and it works. Think back five, ten, 15 or 20 years and take a moment to note if you still see things the way you did back then. If you do, then most likely not much has or will change in your life. If you don't, most likely you are growing—creating new experiences and meeting new people. When you *know better*, you can *be better*, but the key is to apply the knowing into everyday, real-life situations.

Just having a "cosmic breakthrough" or "divine intervention" is only part of the equation. Faith without works is dead. Oftentimes, you need to have a breakdown before you get a breakthrough, but knowing it's a part of the growth process keeps things from getting out of hand. You are right where you are supposed to be, given the beliefs and knowing you have made your truth.

Stop Revolving and Start Evolving

This is easier said than done, but worth the effort. You have two basic choices every moment. Choice #1: you can continue what you have been doing—how you see the world, your life, your relationships and current situation—going around and around and around until you are dizzy from the endless circles you create based on what you believe. This is called *revolving*. Most people seek relief in a bottle or pills or simply more of the same things that make them miserable.

Choice #2 is to identify the beliefs that hold you back—pull on your ear and make a weird noise to remind you that you are slipping backwards—and then do something different. *Evolving* is about moving forward based on the new "knowing" that you have developed out of the experiences you have created by seeing the world, your life, relationships, and situations in a different light.

The deal is that whatever truth you decide will guide your life is ultimately your God. For some people, money is everything. That's why their greed supersedes their religious teachings. For some people, sex is everything, and it supersedes their marriage vows. For some, drugs are everything, and they override their body's natural ability to function. So there really is only one question: which do you prefer—truth or consequences?

CHAPTER 6

Now Is All You Get

*Life is made of millions of moments, but we live
only one of these moments one at a time.
As we begin to change this moment, we begin to
change our lives.*

—Trinidad Hunt

Science has yet to adequately define exactly what constitutes a
moment. Sometimes it's called the present, a minute space of
time, or an instant. Outside of the lab, you know in your soul
when you have experienced a *real moment,* such as seeing your
children for the very first time or when your eyes locked with someone
who returned your gaze and something inside changed forever. A
moment, while hard to define, is one of the most precious building
blocks of life we have. One of humanity's shortcomings is that we think
we have an infinite supply of moments, so we put off the letters we
should write, the people we should call, the love we should be making,
or the walks we should be taking. Whoever said, "there is always tomorrow" should be hung up by their Buster Browns! There is no guarantee
that you will be here in five minutes, much less in 24 hours.

After surviving severe electrical shock treatments at age 19, being cut out of a car at 27, and giving up a kidney to my daughter at 43, I am well aware of the ultimate truth. The sands of time are shifting.

I could have easily put Walter Payton under any and all of the principles of common sense in this book that create an uncommon life. Drive, tenacity, belief in one's ability, and persistence were his trademarks. Walter's Chicago Bear records from 1975 through 1987 are long and impressive. While primarily a running back, Walter could also surprise defenses by throwing the ball.

He was the NFL Player of the Year and Most Valuable Player in both 1977 and 1985. His list of accomplishments includes catching 492 passes for 4,538 yards and 15 touchdowns, and passing 34 times for 331 yards and 8 touchdowns.

Walter's historical career as a running back helped to establish him as the all-time leader in running and combined net yards. Walter contributed 16,726 rushing yards with 100 touchdowns during his tenure with the Bears. He was a first-round draft choice from Jackson State, played in nine Pro Bowls, held the single game rushing record of 275 yards against Central Division rival Minnesota Vikings, and ran for over 100 yards in 77 games.

While always being the number-one target of defensive opponents, Walter missed only one game in his career—due to a bruised thigh in his rookie season—and he went on to play 186 consecutive games. Listed at 5'10" and 202 pounds, he hit like he weighed twice as much and used a stiff arm to destroy any defensive players who stuck their nose in his business. Bears coach Mike Ditka said that Walter was the most complete player he had ever seen. I don't think you could find many who could or would argue with "Da Coach."

In 1998, Walter continued his many philanthropic works through his Walter Payton Foundation. Through his personal involvement and devotion to children's causes, he eased the suffering of many of our nation's neediest children. That is how our paths first crossed.

I had been working on a magazine project with a former Chicago Bear player and met Walter in 1993. After the magazine moved to another state, I approached Walter to work on some of his projects, namely a lithograph that would help raise money for the Payton Foundation. For a year and a half, I had the chance to observe what made him not only "Sweetness" (his nickname), but also "Greatness." On a weekly and sometimes daily basis, I observed the many characteristics of Walter that made him a successful athlete and businessman. He had the ability to take every single moment and make it his own. He bent time to fit his energy, and anyone within arm's reach was on the receiving end of a bear hug, ear flick, or neck rub. Walter defined what "being in the present" is all about.

After a successful launch of the lithographs, I had the opportunity to connect Walter with the World Wrestling Entertainment (WWE) organization. Years of playing in celebrity golf tournaments somehow always pays off—and this was no exception. One of the magazine's advertisers was ICOPRO—a supplement company and a subsidiary of WWE. I had hooked them up with Walter's celebrity golf tournament and have great memories on the links with "The Million Dollar Man" Ted DiBiase, my long-time friend "Mr. Universe" Tom Platz, and the late "Mr. Perfect" Curt Henning. One thing led to another, and in short order I was the linchpin in securing Walter Payton's appearance at a major wrestling extravaganza.

The first event ever held at the United Center in Chicago was not a Bulls game, but a World Wrestling Entertainment event. The WWE had approached Walter about being a guest referee and opening the show because of his huge popularity with the fans of Chicago. We worked out the details, and in just a few days the WWE was shooting promos at Walter Payton, Inc. You should have seen the outtakes on these shots—unforgettable! There was a big build-up on TV, and on the night of the event my wife Jackie and I met Walter and his son Jarrett at the United Center. We went backstage to get ready for the match, and they were all there—the biggest names in wrestling—but they turned into gawking youngsters when "Sweetness" walked down the underground tunnel. Walter signed autographs and took pictures, met wives and kids—he was the main event before the main event even started!

The plan was for Walter to stay outside the ropes and direct and distract the opponents so his guy (Razor Ramone, as I recall) could win. But inside I knew that Walter could not stay outside the ropes—it was not in his nature. We headed to the locker room where Walter handed Jackie his watch and wallet and flipped upside-down against the wall as I held his ankles while he did inverted pushups. Then we put on his jersey and taped the sleeves so his biceps bulged like those of a superhero and sent him out to "do battle." And sure enough, to the fans' delight and true to form, Walter leaped over the ropes near the end of the match and made sure that his guy won. So much for following the script! Eighteen thousand people rose to their feet in appreciation for the man who gave every Chicagoan a reason to cheer for 13 years. Thousands of flashbulbs illuminated the stadium capturing the *moment*.

After the match, Walter said, "Let's go meet some people!" and he led Jackie and me around the huge, new arena. The three of us boarded an elevator and went up to the skyboxes where Walter proceeded to stick his head into every single one. He had to connect with people. And they needed him. After a while we made our way into the kitchen where the chef promptly grilled the best steak I have ever eaten, and the three of us ate in the corner of the kitchen. An hour earlier, Walter had been wowing the crowd—and now he was clowning with the kitchen staff! He was great at creating *moments*.

When the night was over, Jackie and I were leaving to grab a cab home, but before I could even think of walking out front into the thousands of people clamoring outside the stadium, Walter grabbed me, gave me a hug, and said, "Get in, I'll give you guys a ride." So along with Walter's son Jarrett (and about five hundred bucks worth of WWE stuff), we jumped in the limo and out into the street—with hands all over the car windows and shouts of "Walter, we love you!" echoing in the night. It was a moment I will never forget. The limo pulled up in front of our house. Walter grabbed my shoulders and said thanks, gave Jackie a kiss on the cheek, and then told the driver to find a fast-food joint. As they drove down the street, both Jarrett and Walter stuck those giant foam hands with a pointing finger that says "We're #1" on them out the window. It was a fitting end to a great day.

Walter had a special connection with children, and I believe that it's because kids know instinctively what moments are really all about. To this day, every time I give a piece of hard candy to my son Andy, I think of another moment that will live in my mind and heart forever.

It was not unusual for me to take Andy along if I had a meeting with Walter or his assistant, Ginny. Andy was only 3, and often my only choice was to have him tag along. One day while I was standing in the doorway of Ginny's office with Andy holding my right hand, I happened to glance to my right and saw Walter holding out a "hard candy" for Andy—but he was lying on the floor! Only his head and arm were out of his office, and as soon as Andy started toward the door for the candy, *poof!* Walter darted back into his office like a shot. Andy cautiously crept down the hall, and just as he reached the candy Walter had left out on the carpet, Walter grabbed him and the two of them disappeared into his office, laughing like hyenas.

Ginny and I had our meeting, and 20 minutes later I walked into the office of the NFL's all-time leading rusher—the most feared running back to ever carry a pigskin, the man who used a straight arm like a sledgehammer—to find him playing on the floor with my son. They had taken 12 golf tees and set them up like bowling pins, and were using his logo golf balls to mow them down. Unbelievable.

Moments. To this day, when Andy sees a "hard candy," he looks at me and says one word: "Walter."

There was a letter on Walter's wall that I read nearly every time I was in his office. It was from two young parents who had written to Walter to thank him for stopping by to see their terminally ill son. The boy was 10 years old, and Walter came in unannounced, held the hand of the little boy, and stroked his head while he shared his faith in God with the parents. He kissed the boy's forehead and left. A few days later, the boy passed away. The parents wanted Walter to know that it meant the world to them that he had taken the time to stop. That was Walter Payton. But you would also find him answering the office phone in some fake high-pitched voice or playing computer games at the front desk. These are just a few of the many memories I have of Walter, like his celebrity roast, the meetings when he flicked peanuts behind his back to break the tension in the room, or watching him hit a golf ball like a pro. But there is also great regret.

After I had moved to Michigan, I went back to Chicago for a visit. I had not seen Walter for a couple of years, and I went to the office on a Friday. The guard at the front desk recognized me and informed me that the office had moved. I got the address and planned on stopping by to say hi. When I hit the first traffic light, I decided to turn right, go to another appointment, and stop at Payton's on the way back. I became busy, so I didn't stop. I never saw him in person again.

There was a massive outpouring of love when Walter was diagnosed with bile duct cancer. Total strangers offered a part of themselves as organ donors; others held prayer vigils; thousands of letters of support poured in from every corner of the world. Perhaps the most jarring moment was when Walter appeared on national television along with Jarrett and asked for our prayers. We watched the man of steel fall prey to the ravages of cancer right before our eyes.

One year after I made my decision at that traffic light, Walter Payton was gone at the age of 45. It was another reminder that the moment at hand is the only thing that you really own. No one could have predicted that Walter would not see Jarrett play in the NFL or walk Brittany down the aisle or celebrate his 25th wedding anniversary with his wife Connie. Time is the one commodity that you can never get enough of.

Connie Payton has picked up right where Walter left off. She has become an ambassador for children in need and works tirelessly to build the foundation so she can reach more kids than ever before. Connie continues to focus on what she considers her most important obligation: working closely with the Illinois Department of Children and Family Services. The foundation hosts a Holiday Giving Program that provides thousands of gifts for needy children during the holidays year after year, and is currently its largest program. In December 2002, the Holiday Giving Program reached out to 20,000 children. Every August, the Back to School Drive is sponsored by the foundation to provide school supplies to children to help them start the school year with everything they need to succeed.

I made a pledge to myself after Walter died to follow his example—to live every moment to the absolute fullest, even if it's a difficult one. When you start making an effort to recognize the ground you stand on or the way the moon floats through the clouds on a summer night, or the smell of rain on a spring morning, the moment comes alive of its own accord as if it was simply waiting for you to catch up. It's at that point you realize on some level you are supposed to be here.

Go back and check your biology books—nature does not make mistakes! You survived as the one sperm that beat out 900 million others that were all trying to live *your* life. *You* are the result of the one that made it upstream and allowed you entry into into a series of moments called Life. When I see the second hand on the clock tick away, my thoughts always turn to the man who made moments unforgettable, and it reminds me that tomorrow is promised to no one.

Never die easy. Don't let up until you hear the final blow of that whistle. Everything in life is worth fighting for. Leave no regrets.

—Walter Payton

It's a Matter of Moments

Just like the person who punches a clock to start his shift, your card has already been pulled from the rack and punched in, and the meter is running. How much time do you think you have? Since the beginning of time, nearly 70 billion humans have inhabited the Earth at one time or another. At present there are only about 6 billion here. That means 64 billion have been born, have lived their lives, and are gone—most as if they had never been here at all. I hate to be the bearer of reality, but the truth is we are all getting our cards punched out at some point, and our shift will be over.

The average life expectancy in America is just about 77 years, give or take a few. That's just over 28,000 days in which to figure out why you are here, what you are going to do about it, and how you want to live. And just so we are clear, the ground rule is this: life is not fair in any way, shape, or form. You could be here one day and gone the next without any warning. You could do all the "right" things, like exercising, eating right, getting enough sleep, not smoking, and limiting your alcohol intake, and then get struck by lightning, run over by a bus, gored by a bull, or slip in the shower. Life begins in an instant and often ends the same way.

Our arrogance and ego keep us from staying in the moment. We look at the obituary page and cannot imagine our picture there— death is something that happens to someone else, no matter how many funerals we attend. We cannot imagine our own demise, which in turn keeps us from experiencing life to the fullest. *Denial* is not just a river—it's a state as well—one that most of us live in when it comes to understanding that we come in on time and leave on time, and that the in-between time is always the right time to make time for the people, places, and events that are really important.

So, how can you live every moment fully as Walter Payton did? Here's how to get started.

Make a Time Line

Nothing wakes up the ego like a good, swift kick in the cosmic groin, if you will. The ego—that part of us that refuses to think we are connected to everyone else in some way—hates to see proof that someday it will no longer be running the show. Too bad—try this exercise anyway. Hold a sheet paper and then take a pencil and draw a horizontal line. At the left end, put the number 1. Print "50" around the middle of the line, and then "100" at the far right end. Let's say that 1 is your first birthday, 50 denotes the half-century mark, and, if you are really lucky and make it to the Smuckers showcase with Willard Scott, then you will be a centenarian. Now find your age on the time line. Where are you? Do you have more yesterdays than tomorrows? How many really important moments have you missed? How many more will you skip unless you get off the bench and on to the playing field?

Do the Math

If you thought the above experiment was eye-opening, wait until you pull out your trusty old calculator. There are 365 days in our calendar year. The average life expectancy is 77.6 years, so here is your equation: $365 \times 77.6 = 28{,}324$. If you are, let's say, 47 years old, you have racked up 17,155 days behind you and have 11,169 days to go—that's if all the stars line up and you don't take that Great Barrier Reef shark-diving vacation. Every single day that has passed contained moments you missed. The numbers don't lie: you are running out of time—literally.

It's About Time

Keeping the above numbers in mind, know that creating moments that matter is about quality, not quantity. A few names you might recognize did their "work" in a relatively short period of time. Jesus Christ transformed the world in just 12,045 days. Joan of Arc lived only 6,935 days. Martin Luther King Jr. gave us a dream in just 14,235 days. Dian Fossey showed us gorillas in the mist in 19,345 days. John F. Kennedy asked not what our country could do for us but rather what we could do for our country in 16,790 days, and Walter Payton held us in the palm of his hand for a mere 16,425 days.

While days are easy to measure, moments are not. But rather than waiting for moments to come floating along, we need to get about the business of creating them. I have some suggestions. Take a day off from work, surprise your kids, and goof off the entire day. Drop by your wife's place of employment unannounced and tell her how much she means to you. Pick up the phone and call that person you have been meaning to connect with but were too busy to get it done. Sit and watch the sunset or the moonrise. Walk on the lawn early in the morning when the dew still clings to the grass. Turn off all your electronic devices for three hours and take a nap. None of these things will add any years to your life, but they will, without question, *add life to your years*. And that is the only thing you can control—in this moment.

Play Bigger Than You Are

Walter Payton was not the biggest, fastest, or strongest, but he convinced himself that, no matter what, he would score. Playing big from the inside out will magnify the moments of your life. "Big" does not refer to stature, but rather to spirit, fortitude, and attitude. The best way to bring forth your "bigger self " is to stretch past the present limitations imposed by your "smaller self." That begins with how you see your circumstances. Are you locked in or locked out? Can you find a way through, or is every day a dead end? Do you move forward no matter how many times you get knocked down, or do you stay down? When everyone else has given up, do you put in the extra effort to find out what you are made of, or is it easier to throw in the towel? Humans are creatures of habit—and both winning and losing are habits. They are simply points on the continuum of life. Remember that victory and defeat are temporary. Competition to become your best is the only thing that is ongoing until the game is over.

Never Die Easy

Every single day the media shows us why we should be afraid to get out of bed. Turn off the TV and get about your business. The world is full of people worrying about how they are going to die—from what disease or accident, the victim of some stalker or freak event. Don't be afraid of dying. Be terrified of not being fully alive while you have the chance. There are mountains to climb, books to write, diseases to cure, and hands to hold. If not by you, then by whom? And if not now . . . when?

CHAPTER 7

Brailling the World

Curiosity is the bridge that crosses the river of indifference.

—John St.Augustine

I like being alive. Sure, there are days when I wonder if my karma ran over my dogma, but I can recall only a couple of times when getting out of bed did not seem worth the effort. Those days have been far outweighed by the splendor that life continually deposits at my door. The concept of life grows on me more and more each passing moment. I really have led a charmed life—and so have you if you take a really hard look at the connect-the-dots that brought you to where you are today. Good or bad is not important; it's your perception of things that matters. The life force is always moving us in the direction of lessons to be learned, and the sooner you get it, the sooner you go to the next level.

As you've probably realized by now, our lives are pretty short in comparison with redwood trees, the Galapagos tortoise, and re-runs of *Gilligan's Island*. The world we live in is a pretty big place with amazing things to see and even more amazing people with whom to connect. On average, we follow pretty much the same route as those who have come before us, without giving much thought to what else is out there waiting to be discovered. At my last high-school reunion, there were a lot of "got married, bought a house, and had kids" descriptions in the space marked "accomplishments." Of course, there is nothing wrong with the aforementioned items except that marriages often don't last, houses come and go, and kids grow up and move away. We all hear the call of the world, beckoning us to come out and see the miracles before we are gone, but we are either too busy or too afraid to answer. Sometimes, someone has to remind us of what the world has to offer—someone like Bill Kurtis.

You know the voice. Millions tune in to watch Bill Kurtis on *Cold Case Files, Investigative Reports,* and *American Justice* on the A&E Television Network. His award-winning science documentary series *The New Explorers* has become a powerful tool for students globally. For 40 years, he has been at the forefront of breaking news and information that play a crucial role in our lives. He is an explorer, rancher, entrepreneur, and world traveler. He has an incredible sense of humor and an insatiable curiosity that is essential for success. And make no mistake about it, Bill Kurtis is successful. He defines the term "Renaissance man."

Kurtis began his television career as a part-time anchorman in Topeka, Kansas. On a hot June night in 1966, a severe thunderstorm southwest of town was heading straight toward Topeka. Bill got on the air and warned viewers: *"For God's sake, take cover!"* He remained on the air 24 hours straight to cover the event. This warning became synonymous with the destruction that left 16 dead and injured hundreds more, but it was also Bill Kurtis' big moment. That tape was shown all over the country, and his reporting style and ability to remain unfazed in the midst of the devastation caught the eyes of TV executives in Chicago. Despite passing the Kansas bar exam and securing a job with a law firm in Wichita, Bill opted for a career as a broadcast journalist and moved to Chicago in 1966 to work at WBBM-TV as a reporter, eventually anchoring the news.

In 1982, he moved to New York to anchor the CBS Morning News, but returned to Chicago just three years later to the anchor desk at WBBM. Once in Chicago he began to produce documentaries that aired on WTTW, the Chicago PBS station, to rave reviews and widespread acclaim. He started a production company in 1990 and became part of the A&E Television Network in 1991. The success of shows like *Cold Case Files* and *Investigative Reports* put Bill Kurtis into millions of homes and earned him legions of fans.

In 1989, John Denver was scheduled for an event to be held at the Chicago Theater called "Higher Ground." It was not a concert, but rather a unique one-man presentation that John did in a few cities across the country that summer to focus awareness on environmental issues. I was planning to attend the show and had helped to set up some of the media for John's visit. I looked forward to his program that night and the private reception afterward.

As I recall, about a thousand people attended the show, and the seating was first-come, first-served. I grabbed a seat about five rows back in the center and waited for things to get moving. Not more than a few moments went by before I heard a very familiar voice, "Excuse me. Is this seat taken?" It was the unmistakable golden tone of Bill Kurtis. I invited him to sit, we made small talk, and before long John came out and did his thing. Some people who thought it would be a concert were a little disappointed; John sang a few songs, but he really presented his thoughts about the state of the environment, the role humans play, and what actions could be taken to create a sustainable future. It was a moving event, and I left feeling a bit more empowered about making changes in my life.

The next day, for whatever reason, I decided to call Bill at WBBM and get his feedback on the show. I was nowhere near the media at that point, except as a viewer, and had no real interest in journalism or even radio for that matter. I was back in college after a long ten-year gap, and I thought the future for me was pretty well set: I would be a physical education teacher and football coach. Turns out that another plan was in place, and Bill was part of it.

Bill was very cordial in conversation and had some thoughts on the event. They ranged from "I am not sure how you really motivate people to become more aware" to "It's amazing to me that so many people in Chicago would come to hear John Denver speak and not sing." I took the conversation as one of those "followed up on that thought" deals and left it hanging on the phone hook as soon as the call ended. Little did I know at the time that I would eventually move into radio, and that Bill Kurtis would become such a prominent mentor in my life.

A wonderful woman in his office, Joan Dry, would also play an important role in the success of my show.

I had been on the air for only a few months when the thought came to invite Bill on the show. He remembered me from nearly nine years before, and it was quite the on-air conversation. I asked him about his passion for the earth and its inhabitants. He bluntly replied, *"I'm doing God's work."* He said it so matter-of-factly that I repeated the question, and he answered the same way. I did not expect this broadcasting icon, attorney, and rancher to say that he was doing God's bidding. After the show, I sent a copy of the tape to Kurtis Productions for review. A few days later, I got a call from Chicago. It was Joan Dry, Bill's publicist. "I have never heard him say that he is doing 'God's work'!" said Joan. It was to be the first of many phone calls between Kurtis Productions and Eclipse Broadcasting over the next few years. Every single time I meet Bill for lunch or just hang out at the office, I am struck by the insatiable curiosity that keeps Bill Kurtis on the road, bringing us the world via television.

One of the first-hand experiences that showed me not only Bill's curiosity, but also his conviction that human beings have a profound impact on the planet, happened right in my own backyard. Bill had traveled the world for about a year, taking video footage from different critical points on the planet—indicators that the Earth is going through a transition. From all the footage, data, and miles, he aired a special broadcast called "Earth in the Hot Seat," solely from a journalistic point of view—no politics, no hidden agenda, and no fundraising for an unidentified nonprofit. He was just presenting what he witnessed and letting the world decide. I asked Bill to come to Michigan and present the program. He did just that.

As I prepared to introduce Bill that night, my mind raced back to 1990 at the Chicago Theater. It was some kind of fate or destiny that put Bill and me in seats next to each other. Now here it was ten years later: John is gone, and I'm introducing Bill Kurtis to an audience of 500 people. I remember thinking to myself, *How do things like this happen?*

Bill introduced the program that we were about to be viewed, and then he and I retired to the pressroom to take questions. About an hour later, the show ended, and he took the podium to get feedback from the audience. The first hand shot up. "Mr. Kurtis, with all due respect, everything you are talking about is garbage. I have been work-ing in the woods for 20 years, and I've never seen any of the stuff you are talking about. I think it's all propaganda, and global warming is a liberal agenda."

Bill looked directly at the man and simply said, "Thank you," and then turned to take the next question. The man stood there not quite knowing what to do, and my first thought was, *there is incredible power in detachment*. For the previous hour, the audience had seen images of leaning utility poles that we had anchored in permafrost that was melt-ing. Because of the warmer weather, a certain type of beetle was destroy-ing trees year round. The ecosystem was off-kilter, and the information Bill had gathered alarmed some and caused others to rely on old para-digms. ("The planet is billions of years old, and my 20 years in the woods qualifies me to call the shots.") Still, others asked what they could do in their own way to be more aware.

Behind all of it—the contents of the film, the journey north from Chicago to Michigan, the years Bill has adventured around the world swimming with dolphins, peeking into eagles' nests, or interviewing drug lords—is Bill's insatiable curiosity. It is a natural part of the human design, but something that unfortunately most of us lose around the age of 12. For Bill Kurtis, that curiosity has intensified over the years, not lessened.

When Bill goes on television after doing his globe-trotter routine, he stirs the pot of curiosity for his audience that is so essential to liv-ing an uncommon life. He took the first step in the heroic journey—he did it for himself, for the part of him that needs to seek truth—and now he takes the rest of us along for the ride.

As a mentor in the business of media, Bill has been a beacon to follow in a very difficult industry for me personally. On one of my visits back to Chicago, Bill and I stepped out for a burger at one of his favorite neighborhood establishments. During the course of the conversation about the nuances of the human experience, he moved his plate right to the edge of the table and said, "Life is all about being curious enough to take things right to the edge and then watching to see what happens." I figure if it has worked for Bill, who am I to disagree?

I have to take a moment to mention an absolutely amazing woman named Megan Murphy, Bill's lead person at Kurtis Productions. She is one of the most astute people I have ever met when it comes to seeing all sides and more to whatever challenge may be on tap. Megan's power comes from the fact that she knows who she is and where she is headed. Her friendship and Friday afternoon conversations have been a very important part of my work, and it was upon her recommendation and Bill's confidence in my vocals that I was given the opportunity to voice over a program on the History Channel called "High-Tech Lincoln" in 2005. The show was about the Abraham Lincoln Library and Museum that had just opened in Springfield, Illinois. The chance to work with the pros at Kurtis and move out of radio and into the television medium was great. It was a kick to turn on the TV and watch the show—with my voice all over it. And to think that it all started back in 1990 by choosing a seat in the theater.

Just like all the other people in this book, Bill Kurtis walks his talk, whether he is refurbishing a small Kansas town to the look of the 1880s, developing grass-fed cattle that will benefit steak lovers, cracking some *Cold Case* file, or accepting gifts from a tribe in Africa. It makes me think of the childhood book, *Curious George*, about the man with the big yellow hat and how much his little monkey George learned from his curiosity. Because of his curiosity, Bill Kurtis has taught millions the magic of wonder and how important it is to not only believe in what we see, but to cherish it as well. And speaking of yellow things, since this is a tell-all book, I figure one little secret leaked won't hurt his career at this point: Bill Kurtis is addicted to . . . marshmallow Peeps®—those little sugar bombs that pop up right before Easter. I also freely admit I have enabled his habit on more than one occasion. (I only buy them; I never actually eat them.) I have even had friends stuff them in his mailbox when I could not get down to do the deed myself. It's just my way of feeding his habit . . . and saying thanks.

So the next time you click on the tube and see the man with the silver hair and inquisitive eyes, take a moment and think about the miles he has traveled to do what he can to make the world a better place for those who follow. He is driven by his curiosity to work in the service of life and the living, in search of the answers to questions unknown. He sees the world not only for what it is, but for what it also could be. What a wonderful way to go through life!

You have to be curious enough to go upstream and find the source. When you find the source, the truth is revealed. And then you can invite others to do the same. It's what we've come here to do."

—Bill Kurtis

Are You Lost? No, Just Curious

The world is a living, breathing organism in which we are just one cast member in a show that contains billions of bit-part players. There is a great dance going on, and it's not the lambada! The world in which we live is filled with mysteries waiting to be solved, treasures to be found, and secrets deep in the forests and oceans of our planet that have yet to be revealed. When I was a kid, I couldn't wait for *The Undersea World of Jacques Cousteau* to come on the tube. It was my chance to see what was going on in places I could only dream of visiting. Those shows stoked the curiosity of a generation. But then we got busy and added cable, had kids, and got a "real" life. The Curious George in us sat in a tree eating bananas, watching reality shows, and getting fat.

Curiosity is technically defined as "the desire to know," and without it humanity would never have gotten out of the cave or created the wheel or lifted off the ground at Kitty Hawk or gone to the moon and beyond. It is one of our greatest gifts and strengths that have lapsed into a "curiosity coma" as we have begun to spend less time in the wonders of nature and more time watching hand-picked contestants wallow around on some remote island vying for a million bucks.

Wise old Socrates insisted, "The unexamined life is not worth living." The only way that you can examine your existence, despite all the odds of being born, the near misses you have survived, and the incredible notion that humans above all other creatures have the opportunity to literally change their experience of life, is to resurrect your curiosity quotient and bring back the Technicolor dreams of yesterday. Then, the movie of your life—*starring you*—becomes the blockbuster hit it was meant to be.

You don't have to crawl over Aztec ruins or dive in a mini-sub to the ocean depths to appreciate the wonders of the world. A new, exciting, and expanding world is right under your feet—if you are curious enough to seek it.

Close Your Eyes

This chapter is called "Brailling the World" for a reason. Most of us have become so immune to the fabric and texture of life that our senses have become impotent. When was the last time you took a walk in the rain without an umbrella? How about strolling through the forest (or city park) without answering your cell phone or listening to your iPod? Even if you are a city dweller, you can regain a bit of your senses by shutting off one of them. Find a safe place—even your living room will do—and close your eyes for five minutes. Resist the temptation to open them and see what is going on. Just listen. Before long, your curiosity gene will start to kick in and bring to you a world that has been ignored—and surrounds you every day.

Dig a Hole

Literally, when was the last time you had some dirt under your fingernails? For most of us, the ground on which we walk is something to fertilize, plow, pave, or shovel. Just beneath the first couple layers of grass, rock, and stone, another world exists. If drilling is not an option, find a flagstone or brick to uproot. Check out what kind of activity is going on without regard to your human existence. We think we have dominion over everything until we remember this fact: there are five major themes in the biodiversity of the Earth. First, there is the plant life in all its forms, from the mighty redwoods to the smallest ferns and lichens. Second, there is the animal life in all its forms, which includes *everything* that swims, crawls, walks, and flies. Third is the water world—the amazing system that is the lifeblood of the planet—the oceans, lakes, streams, ponds, and the aquifer that feeds it all. Fourth, there is the geology of the Earth itself—the rocks, minerals, stones, sand, and dirt that hold this amazing little blue ball in space together. Fifth is the human race with all its potential and problems—just over 6 billion people, with more showing up every day. Now here is the kicker: the first four don't need us to survive, *but we need the other four in order to survive.*

Change the View

Because we are creatures of habit and don't like to break from the routine (even that which isn't very good for us), find simple ways to change the way you see things. Drive a different way to work. Park in a spot farthest from the door at the supermarket and, while you are making your way across the parking lot, notice the things lying on the ground: money, old lottery tickets, and keys, whatever. Doing something different forces your brain to consider new options and ways of seeing the world in which you live. Set the alarm an hour early and just listen to the birds greet the day. Stay up an hour later (with the television off) and just sit. All of these little ways of increasing your sense of curiosity will become a new habit and help you to construct a different pattern that makes each day more unique.

Take Something Apart

I remember Emmett, the "fix-it man," on the old *Andy Griffith Show*. He was always pulling apart a toaster or clock to get it up and running again. In these days of a "throw-it-away-if-it-doesn't-work" mentality, set aside a couple of hours and find something to pull apart and put back together (making sure, of course, that it's not plugged in). If that doesn't work for you, go buy a model airplane or birdhouse or kite kit and build something. Engaging our hands and minds in how things work and are constructed is a good way to keep the Curious George inside alive. The very powerful question of "How does this work?" opens all sorts of avenues to explore. Once you break it down, putting it back together is a sure way to keep you interested—if not humble. And don't get frustrated . . . it's not allowed!

Ask Better Questions

I have been interviewing people for years based on one simple question: "Why do you do what you do?" Find someone you think you know and play talk-radio host. Do an interview with him or her. Ask about their heritage, dreams, and goals. Ask about their plans for the future, why they live where they do, and what five things are most important to them. Engage them in conversation that goes beyond "How's the weather?" or "What's for dinner?" Each of us has a lifetime of experiences we are waiting to share, to examine, and to reveal. We are truly universes unto ourselves and don't even realize it most of the time.

And if none of the above suggestions works for you, find a really tall tree with an eagle's nest and climb up for a good look inside. If nothing else, the view will definitely change—and that is the whole point!

CHAPTER 8

It's about Closing
the Gaps

Life shrinks or expands in proportion to one's
courage.

—Anaïs Nin

Growing up in Chicago, I was taught from an early age to hate the Green Bay Packers. Every year when the Bears and Packers would meet, the TV set would get turned up loud, and words I only heard on Sundays between noon and three were shouted even louder. The Bears of the '60s had little in the way of winning records, but they were the Monsters of the Midway—Dick Butkus, Gale Sayers, Doug Atkins, Doug Buffone, and Ronnie Bull. While there was not much to cheer about, there was always the chance that Butkus was going to knock off someone's block—a cause for major celebration in the Windy City.

I have cousins who live in the Fox Valley of Wisconsin, and every summer vacation was spent in the northern regions of Cheese Land. Uncle Ronnie and my dad would go back and forth about who was going to come out on top in the upcoming season. At times, the Packers were the cream of the NFL crop, with Vince Lombardi at the helm, and a supporting cast with names like Bart Starr, Willie Davis, Jimmy Taylor, Ray Nitschke, and Forrest Gregg.

Those were the days when our heroes were much closer to us than today. They were not the glittery multi-millionaires with private jets and agents. They were the men we hoped to be some day—guys who did their thing because they loved the game and the respect it earned them from their peers. They played with every injury you can think of. Deacon Jones, famed L.A. Rams defensive end, talked about playing with broken fingers, a wrenched back, ulcerated eyeballs, and a bloody mouth—*all in one game!* These iron men displayed courage with teamwork and cunning as pro football was finding its way into America's living rooms. I'm privileged to be the friend of one member of this stellar cast.

Born in Jordan, Idaho, the family moved to Sandpoint, Idaho when Jerry Kramer was in the fourth grade. Jerry had always dreamed of playing football for the Los Angeles Rams—but first he had to overcome some overwhelming circumstances. When he was a kid, he accidentally shot himself in the right forearm with a 10-gauge shotgun, severing nerves, leaving him with a fist that could never quite close and a huge chunk missing from his forearm. Another time, he was chasing a calf and ran full-speed into a splintered plank, sending giant splinters into his groin. It wasn't until years later when doctors feared he had cancer that they discovered four forgotten large slivers of wood lodged in his intestines that caused internal bleeding and tumors. At one point, his condition was so grave that it was rumored Jerry had passed on. He had broken his neck, ribs, and leg playing football. He suffered from brain concussions and a detached retina. He'd gone through a car windshield and fallen two stories from a bell tower. Two massive scars ran up the back of his neck, for which his teammates called him "Zipperhead."

Yet despite these seemingly insurmountable obstacles, he was the most celebrated offensive guard in the history of the NFL. Jerry played his first game in 1958, the same year I was born. For ten seasons he became part of the Lombardi legacy, leading those murderous power sweeps with guard Fuzzy Thurston for running back Paul Hornung and fullback Jimmy Taylor. He ended his career in 1968 and became a best-selling author. *Instant Replay: The Green Bay Diary of Jerry Kramer* was the first time fans caught a glimpse behind the scenes of pro football with arguably the greatest NFL team ever to take the field—Vince Lombardi's Packers. It chronicled the 1967 run to the Super Bowl and

the ups and downs of being a pro athlete. Honest, open, and question-
ing, it has become a classic. I was on a family vacation to Appleton
back in 1968 when a life-long game of connect-the-dots began and put
Jerry Kramer in my orbit.

At some point during our vacation, my dad must have needed a
shave. When he bought a Personna, "The Electro-Coated Blade," it
came with a premium gift: the book *Instant Replay*.

I was 10 that year, and I stretched out in the back seat of my dad's
1959 Chevy Impala and read the entire book on the three-hour ride
back home to Chicago. Thirty-seven years later, I still read that original
copy every autumn. If you would have told me on that summer vacation that Jerry Kramer would become a close friend and teacher in my
life, I would have said, "No way." But the universe always finds a way.
It leaves no gaps.

In the late '80s, I connected with a former Chicago Bear and co-
created a magazine called *Pro Athlete Insider*. As we were putting
together an advisory board, one name immediately popped into my
head. If there was an athlete who understood the importance of this
project and what it would take to make it work, it was Jerry Kramer.
After a lot of digging, I found Jerry Kramer's phone number. He was
living in Idaho. I steadied myself as I prepared to make the call. *What
would I say to him? How could I possibly thank him for being such a big
part of my life?*

I dialed and held my breath. When the phone was picked up on
the other end, a husky voice barked, "This is Jerry."

"Mr. Kramer? I . . . I . . . my name is John, and I . . . uh, just wanted
to thank you for writing *Instant Replay*. Because of that book—and the
way you blocked Merlin Olsen—I learned that I have talents and abilities that I might never have found. I was wondering if you would consider being part of a new magazine that makes sure 10-year-old boys
know how important it is to dream big—even if they hate the Packers."

Jerry laughed. As I remember, that call lasted about a half-hour. He
invited me to a "roast" of Packer defensive end Willie Davis in
Appleton the following weekend. Driving north from Chicago, the
memories came flooding back. Many of the old landmarks were gone:
the Big Boy restaurant on College Avenue had a new name, and the
Dreamland Motel had become condos, and a massive mall now stood
where corn once grew. But none of that mattered because I was going

to spend the evening with Jerry Kramer and the Packers. That trip was a turning point in my life.

The "roast" was a glorious evening—listening to the tales of days gone by from a group of men whom I had only read about. The humility of spirit and the genuine feeling of camaraderie were infectious. We stayed up late listening to war stories—how Max McGee and Paul Hornung sent Lombardi into fits. Or the time that Jerry Kramer tried to tell Frank Sinatra how to sing. We relived the "Ice Bowl" victory over the Dallas Cowboys into the wee hours of the morning.

The next day I drove further north to Green Bay for an event at the Packer Hall of Fame as Jerry's guest. It was Bears–Packers week, and as we sat at the long lunch table, they introduced themselves. It was clear in just a few minutes that I was the only Chicagoan in the room. The man next to me, sitting in a wheelchair and hooked to an oxygen tank, came to life as he described a life-long dedication to the Packers. He vented his hatred of the Bears and Coach Mike Ditka, saying that if he could get out of his wheelchair, he would do unspeakable things to the Bears coach. When he finished, he turned to me and said, "Where are you from, son?" To save my backside in hostile territory, I replied the only way I could: "*Denver!*" Jerry and I have been friends ever since.

Jerry's presence has a staggering effect on people. At one point, I brought Jerry to Upper Michigan to participate in a celebrity fishing tournament, but we also snuck in a day of golf. On the way to the links, we stopped at the house of a man who was in the twilight of his life—and among the thousands who had braved the cold in the "Ice Bowl" against the Dallas Cowboys in 1967. It was an orchestrated stop. As the daughter of the elderly man led us through the garage into the house, I had a unique view from behind Jerry and over his shoulder into the room where the man sat in a chair, hooked up to oxygen. "You're Jerry Kramer!" he cried out in recognition. Jerry simply peered over his glasses and winked. The years and sickness drained from the gentleman on the spot. For nearly a half-hour, Jerry sat near the old man and shared stories of gridiron glory. Jerry had transported them back to yesterday—when they were both young, and the aches, pain, and sickness of old age were not even a thought. Life was good again, if only for a short time. I wondered how many of today's "superstars" would have that kind of effect nearly 40 years after they retired, and I wished that all the sportswriters who vote on Hall of Fame induction could have been there. Sometimes what we do off the field is just as important as what we do on the field.

That night, we drove on the highway near Little Bay de Noc with the windows down singing John Denver's "Some Days Are Diamonds" at the top of our lungs. We didn't think we were too bad, but the fish were reportedly moving in erratic patterns as if some type of sonar waves were running down their nervous system—perhaps it was our fault.

Jerry followed his first book with *Farewell to Football*, and in 1984 another classic, *Distant Replay*, took a look back at the team years later. We live in a sports-crazed society, and I have witnessed first-hand how grown men and women become infatuated with their sports idols. We all know the headlines of athletes who have gone down the tubes, and the millions of dollars that young men and women get paid to play games. For a pro athlete to publicly admit a flaw takes a great deal of courage. In *Distant Replay*, Jerry freely admits that at one time the sound of his own voice was the only music he listened to. Then at some point he realized that he did not know everything and that learning was a full-time process—a bigger game.

Jerry is always talking about closing the gap in life—going from who you are to who you can be. He insists that all of us have the ability and the responsibility to take our lives to the next level. It is what the game of life is all about. He learned a great deal from Vince Lombardi over the years and now feels it is his duty and high honor to carry the message to people hungry for direction. It is a theme that runs through those early heroes of football—the young men now in their '60s and '70s who gave fans all over America so much to cheer about and so much to learn.

Jerry has been successful in great part due to the beliefs he has developed and his courage to live by a code of honor of teamwork. He looks at life as a game and the human race as a team on which we all play. Teams need a great coach to push, remind, and teach. In a time when it's more about *me*, Jerry Kramer reminds us that real winning in life is about *we* and the courage to close the gaps.

A lot of men mistakenly think that courage has to do with not feeling afraid. In a world that is full of reasons to feel fear, courage is the ability to feel the fear and move forward in spite of it. Every now and again, I catch myself thinking of Jerry sitting in his office, a holdover from another time, and I am reminded that his mere presence is an example. In spite of all the operations, setbacks, and disappointments, he keeps moving ahead courageously.

Just a few days ago, I spent a fabulous evening with Jerry and his daughter Diane, his son-in-law Scott, and their children in Green Bay. At one point, his soon-to-be 10-year-old grandson was sitting on the couch between us, listening intently to "Poppa." And then it hit me—he was just about the same age I was when I first read *Instant Replay*. As I headed home the next day—on the very same highway that my folks drove those many summer vacations so long ago—I thought about a young boy reading a book on football in the back of his dad's car, and I remembered dreaming about what it would be like to meet Jerry Kramer. Life had closed another gap.

Most of us are fearful of taking a chance, of making a change, of taking the next step. The only way to cross the goal line is to keep pounding away—running different patterns and having a flexible game plan. Of course, it helps to have someone to run interference, not to mention a great coach. More than a few autumns have passed since the Packer glory years, and last I checked Jerry Kramer is still coming around the corner on a power sweep and closing the gaps. That takes courage.

Basically, it comes down to belief in yourself. Don't be afraid to step out and attempt something that will make you stretch and grow beyond what you thought was possible.

Find the gaps in your life and begin the process of closing them. Each time you do, you are that much closer to your goals.

—Jerry Kramer

Closing the Gaps with Courage

When the subject of courage comes up, many images come to mind—John Wayne heading toward six gunfighters with the reins in his teeth and a blazing Winchester in each fist. What it must feel like as you strap yourself into the space shuttle and head up to the heavens. On September 11, 2001, courage was redefined and revealed by those who went into crumbling buildings looking for just one sign of life. For some people, courage is the ability to swing your legs out of bed just one more morning. It could be a single parent working two jobs to make ends meet. In Jerry Kramer's case, courage is defined as transcending the gap between circumstances and certainty of self—to become all you can be and a role model for others to do the same.

Courage is defined in *Webster's* as "mental or moral strength to venture, persevere, and withstand fear or difficulty." Notice there's no mention of fighting dragons, rescuing a damsel in distress, fighting off Bengal tigers, or any of the other things we have come to associate with courage. Going from where you are to where you want to be is courage defined because it is one of the most challenging journeys you will ever take. It means letting go of who you thought you were (and all that goes with it) and accepting who you can be (and all that goes with it). While most people think Gap is a clothing store, it is also one of the most important "beginning/ending" points in your life. It's a moment that appears to be the end of one path but really is the beginning of another. You may be required to "close minor gaps" several times a day, like fixing the sink, making lunch, getting the kids to school on time, and finishing your college degree online. Or you may need to navigate "major gaps," like a death in the family, relocating due to business, or finding love again. Any change, no matter how small, requires courage.

The interesting thing about courage is that we already have it. Just like the lion in *The Wizard of Oz* who was looking for some outside validation to display his courage, most of us don't even realize the courage we have and how many gaps we have closed in our lives up to this point. After speaking with and to thousands of people over the past ten years, I can say with all certainty that it's not the place we are that bothers us so much (e.g., wrong job, house, mate, or income), but rather the gaps between where we are and where we think we should be. There is nothing more challenging for the human mind than the freefall that occurs when change takes place. The gap—that space between here and there—is a void often filled with fear. It's also, however, a place of great learning, trust, faith, and patience if you choose to see it that way. Courage to see things in a new way determines to a great extent how long you stay in the gap—and your ability to close it.

Most likely you've never had to put on a helmet and go face-to-face with a Hall of Fame defensive tackle like Merlin Olsen—and hopefully you never will. You can, however, learn to close the gaps in your life from someone who did it better than anyone else in his position in the history of the NFL—Jerry Kramer.

Lead with Your Head

When it comes to making a block or a tackle, at least in the old days, the coaches always told us to lead with our facemask—on both sides of the ball. It accomplishes two things. First, there is nothing like having a 250-pound man sticking his face in your chest to get your attention. Second, where the head goes, the body follows. For our purposes, it's very important to have the courage to stick your face right in whatever gap is on tap. Whether it's the gap between your work and spending time with the kids or the gap between the job you have and going back to college to get your degree, be smart. Lead with your head. One of Kramer's greatest assets is that he was a student of his opponents. Each week for 11 years, there was a new challenge across the line from him trying to get to the quarterback. Be smart about your choices and figure out what needs to change in your sphere of influence to make the gap between here and there smaller.

Know Your Position

With the rodent-like pace most of us keep, it's easy to forget what role or position you play and the assigned duties that go along with it. We are wearing more hats today than ever before; trying to be all things to all people will result in a very watered-down performance. One of the biggest reasons that winning teams continue to win is really very simple: everyone knows what position they play, what they are supposed to do, and then they follow through until they reach the desired result—whether it be a touchdown, selling cars, or raising kids. You don't see very many offensive tackles throwing a football for a 40-yard gain, and conversely it's not often that the quarterback lines up against some cat-quick defensive end. Figure out what you are supposed to do, and then do it. Say no to the things that are not part of your position.

Ignore the Small Hurts

The following is a brief list of Jerry Kramer's "challenges."

- **1950:** Caught shirt in turning screw of lathe at high school. Ripped out a fist-size chunk of right side, requiring stitches.
- **1951:** Accidentally shot right arm and side with double-barrel 10-gauge shotgun. Wound required four operations, skin grafts, and plastic surgery over the next few years.
- **1953:** Ran over sharp board while chasing calf in pasture. Seven-and-one-half-inch-long, three-quarter-inch-thick splinter penetrated groin and lodged in large muscle near spine.
- **1955:** Operation for suspected chipped vertebra in neck results in "zipper" scar.
- **1960:** Brain concussion and detached retina suffered in game against Los Angeles Rams (surgically corrected after the season).
- **1961:** Two bones in left ankle separated and ligaments severely strained during game against the Minnesota Vikings.
- **1964:** Operation for tumor on liver. Emergency colostomy. Six-and-one-half-hour surgery in lower left abdominal area during which four slivers of wood (that had been lodged for 11 years) were removed. Jerry looked so bad after this surgery that even his barber thought he was dead. Missed the entire season.

Now, what ache or pain were you complaining about? You can't close the gaps by focusing on what isn't working.

Check the "Win Column" Often

Despite the above list of Mr. Kramer's supposed "setbacks," he also accomplished the following. The University of Idaho (his alma mater) retired his number (64). He established himself as a star player with the Green Bay Packers, was named All-Pro five times, and was a member of one of the greatest dynasties in the history of pro sports. As an offensive guard, he also kicked extra points. Jerry's kicking of three field goals was the deciding factor in the 1962 Championship win over the New York Giants. He racked up 29 field goals and 90 PATS (points after touchdowns) for a total of 177 points scored.

In 1967, he "closed the gap" with the famous block in the "Ice Bowl" championship game and made NFL history. Two years later, he was voted as the best guard in the first 50 years of pro football. Oh yeah, Jerry wears two Super Bowl rings and also earned a spot on the all-time all-Super Bowl team selected by sportscaster John Madden. He was the first pro athlete/author with the publication of *Instant Replay*, co-authored by the late Dick Schaap. He followed up with *Farewell to Football, Lombardi: Winning Is the Only Thing* and *Distant Replay*, also with Dick Schapp. In 2005, he released his *Inside the Locker Room* CD that is an audio diary of the Lombardi years. During his seasons with the Packers, they won more games than they lost. It was their ability to focus on the winning that made them the most dominant team of the '60s.

So the lesson here again is very simple. When you get knocked down, get up. When you lose, take it as a learning experience. Keep track of your wins, big and small, so if you start to lose focus, you can see what results you've created by closing the gaps that you didn't think you could—but did.

Get in the Game

Abraham Lincoln said, "Things may come to those who wait, but only the things left by those who hustle." Watching the game of your life from the sidelines will not change the outcome, but finding your position and developing a game plan will.

Sports can teach us some great lessons—if we are open to the teachings. From the first time I read *Instant Replay* nearly 40 years ago, I have been implementing the things that I have learned from Jerry— who got them from Lombardi, who got them from his years as one of the "Seven Blocks of Granite" at Fordham University—and the game of touch continues. But it all starts with the courage and honesty to see your life as a game, in which you participate, not observe as a spectator. One thing about life is that you cannot hide very long. Some way, somehow, you will be pulled onto the playing field—and your time in practice will either pay off or not. Closing the gap from yesterday to tomorrow requires that you focus on today. Just for this day, have the courage to see what needs to change in you. Just for today, identify one "gap" in your life that needs to be closed. Just for today, believe that you have the resources, drive, and ability to close that gap. Just for today, see your life as a football game. You get four quarters to play, a few timeouts, and a break in the middle. What quarter are you in? How much time do you have to close the gaps? And if not you, who will? If not today, when? Just get in the game.

CHAPTER 9

Follow the Yellow Brick Road

Whether we name divine presence synchronicity,
serendipity, or graced moment matters little.
What matters is the reality that our hearts have
been understood. Nothing is as real as a healthy
dose of magic which restores our spirits.

—Nancy Long

*T*he *Wizard of Oz* has delighted audiences for years with its simple themes, colorful characters, and brilliant performances. I
have watched it countless times, but it was not until recently
that a very important lesson leapt out at me like a flying monkey. Perhaps what *Oz* is all about is *faith*—learning to let the universe
handle the details and simply putting one foot in front of the other.

It's possible that the reason so many people connect with *The
Wizard of Oz* is that at some point (whether we admit it or not) we see
ourselves in Dorothy, Scarecrow, Tin Man, or the Cowardly Lion. I
know a few talk-radio hosts who feel they are the all-knowing, big-
headed Wizard with all the answers. And we cannot forget Toto, the
Wicked Witch of the West, Glenda the Good Witch, and those wonderful Munchkins. Their journey is our journey. Who has never felt like

running away from the storms of life as Dorothy did? Have you ever worked a job that you hated, stuck in a field with a pole up your backside like Scarecrow? Can you remember a time when circumstances had you rusted in place as the rain did over time to Tin Man? And who among us, like the Cowardly Lion, has ever puffed up and put on a big front to scare away people, knowing all the while that inside we were frightened to death?

Life is filled with Wicked Witches who will try to rob you of your good, Munchkins who will keep you on the path, and trees that throw apples at you if you pick too much. We never tire of watching the movie because deep inside, as we root for Dorothy to get home, Scarecrow to find his brain, Tin Man to get his heart, and Lion to discover his courage, we are hoping the same for ourselves. That is why following the Yellow Brick Road must be by faith, not by sight. It is when you least expect it that a chance meeting can send your life in a whole new direction or give some glimpse into the future to keep you on your personal path to Oz.

When you think of the ONO (One Name Only) Club, a few come to mind—Bono, Cher, Donald—but at the top of the list, of course, would have to be . . . Oprah. Millions of people have connected with her honesty, self-excavation, humor, and ability to bring a message of possibility to talk television—no easy task. A chance meeting in 1986, and another in 1993, were wake-up calls certainly orchestrated by the Wizard himself—and a stepping-stone for "yours truly."

Just two weeks after Jackie and I were married in 1986, a drunk driver hit us broadside the night we picked up our wedding pictures. Lying between two worlds—the here-and-now and the hereafter—I had to be cut from the car. It was only by simple grace that I survived. Experts say that getting married is the most stressful thing you will ever do, but this was "pushing it." At the court hearing a few weeks later, the driver got a slap on the wrist (after leaving the scene of the accident), and that night I experienced anxiety attacks so severe I had to be remanded to Sheridan Road Hospital in Chicago. It was the kind of place where they take your belt and shoelaces, and you are followed around by a couple of guys who look like defensive tackles. At first they thought steroids were making me whacked-out (the White Coats didn't know what time well spent in a gym looks like), but after that was ruled out, they figured that the combination of getting married, having a Lincoln hit me broadside at 70 mph, being cut out of my car, and watching the guy get away with it—not to mention living above a funeral home (my father-in-law was an undertaker) and not being able to work—all combined to put me over the edge. Gee ... ya think? It was most definitely time for a honeymoon.

Jackie was working as a travel agent, and we had been booked on a cruise for some time. We were heading out of Miami on the *Song of America* toward San Juan, St. Thomas, and Puerto Rico. As we began to leave port, I noticed a woman wearing a large hat and sunglasses looking overboard, and while I did not watch much daytime television, it sure looked like Oprah Winfrey to me. Before I could say anything, another woman stepped up and asked to have her picture taken with Ms. Winfrey. As Oprah obliged, her hand somehow caught the cord of the woman's Walkman (remember those?), and it looked like it was going down two stories into the water. Being the vigilant shipmate, I reached to grab it at the same time as Oprah, and somehow her famous finger poked me in the eye. She was aghast while I feigned blindness and agony. After I assured her all was well, we went our separate ways, occasionally running into each other in the gift shop (and once getting a handful of T-shirts lobbed at me by by Oprah in the gift shop after jokingly announcing that *The Color Purple* book on display was much better than the movie). It wasn't until we docked in Puerto Rico that I had the chance to see Oprah looking like a superstar as she walked through the ship's lobby in a stunning silver dress. Of course, it was about the same time that Stedman Graham came on board, but I can't imagine one had to do with the other! It was a great trip all the way around and just what Jackie and I needed. I had no idea I would ever see Oprah in person again.

But the universe had other plans. Seven years later, on a Saturday afternoon, I received a call from my friend Matt Blair, the former Minnesota Viking linebacker. He wanted to know if I could attend a banquet Sunday night and a golf fundraiser on Monday. My first question was about the amount of food to be served (got to have priorities!), but I agreed to join Matt for what I thought would be just another golf outing.

The next day I headed out to the Cantigny Golf Course near Chicago for the event. Turns out, it was a fundraiser for Stedman

Graham's Athletes Against Drugs organization. Major sports stars were attending, along with the "who's who" of business and entertainment. Dressed to the nines, I wandered the adjoining war museum before dinner and connected with the only other person I knew there—former DePaul Blue Demons basketball coach, the legendary Ray Meyer. Even though Stedman is Ms. Winfrey's longtime partner, it never dawned on me that Oprah would be there. Duh.

It was time for the event to begin, and Matt was nowhere to be found. I made sure I was first in line at the banquet table, loaded the appropriate plates with magnificent fare (I knew this was a big deal—the fish still had their heads), and found myself in the main dining room with a full plate and hundreds of open seats. I figured the best plan would be to take a seat in the back, stay out of the way, and wait for Matt to arrive. With my back to the door, I began putting on the feedbag in fine form—I even had the napkin in the right place—and then a feeling came over me, like someone was watching over my shoulder. Expecting to see the headwaiter preparing to ask me to get out of a reserved seat, I spun around to find myself face to face with . . . Oprah—again.

She said, "Is this seat taken?" I glanced at the other 999 empty chairs, and my first thought was something like, *Yeah, they're all taken. You're in the wrong room.* But I stowed my off-the-wall comment and graciously invited her to dine alongside. In moments, Gordon Johnson, the CEO of the Jane Addams Hull House Association, and his wife Deloris joined us. There we sat, the four of us at a table set for ten. No one else took a seat at our table for the entire evening, and did I get the looks! How did I rate? Who was I to be sitting next to Oprah? I wasn't a celebrity per se. My football and sports marketing background was about the only thing I could hang my cleats on. The thought of being a talk radio voice wasn't even in my consciousness. I was not yet fully engaged in my Yellow Brick Road journey, but I was seeking my way to Oz in the process of writing a book, and that's where the conversation began.

"You don't remember me, do you?" I asked.

"No, sorry, I don't," said Ms. O.

"We were on a cruise ship together—seven years ago—well, I was with my wife and you were with Stedman. But you know what I mean," I stammered.

Oprah looked at me like her memory banks were searching for some sort of connection, but instead she just graciously said, "So what are you doing now?"

"Well, right now I am eating."

"Gee, I hadn't noticed. You're pretty good at it. I meant, what are you doing with your life?"

"Been working on a book called *All Are Chosen.*"

"Hmmmm," said Ms. O.

"What does 'hmmmm' mean?"

"That's the truth, isn't it? That we are all chosen in some way, shape, or form."

"Yep. I grew up with the old 'many are called but few are chosen' deal, but after getting a few whacks I realized we are all chosen—we just don't know it."

The dinner progressed. I learned from Gordon about the Hull House Association and the incredible work they do, and the table talk went from who in the room had real hair to television to our views on life. Still no Matt Blair.

Dinner was great and featured more "grilling"—no, not of the steak, but me.

"So, Mr. Inspiration," said Oprah, "what is the greatest lesson you've learned?"

Silence. The room seemed to be a vacuum of nothingness. I gulped between bites and finally said, "It's not what happens that matters; it's only how you respond that counts."

A moment passed, and she said, "You got it."

The table resumed normal breathing. I felt like I had earned a shot at dessert with that answer.

A bit later, another inquisition: "What are you going to do with your time on the planet?"

"Not real sure yet. I need to finish this book and see. . . . "

"Might want to find out. Might want to see how far you can take your gifts. Might want to be the change."

Silence. Something was going on here that was not on the dinner program.

I looked over at Gordon and Deloris, both with eyes wide and jaws agape. I was hoping they would ask me to pass something—potatoes, veggies, gas, anything! But, no relief.

"Well?" said Ms. O, with all the intent that the best-known woman in the world could create.

"Yes, I ... I ... will," I sputtered.

"If you're going to write a book called *All Are Chosen*, you better walk the talk."

"Yes, ma'am."

I felt like I was sitting next to the Great Carnac or something. (For those of you too young to remember, he was a fortune-teller character by Johnny Carson. If you don't know who Johnny Carson was, use the Internet!) I was being visited by either Glenda the Good Witch or a Munchkin or a combination of both when I least expected it—and in a way that I could only begin to understand, but would not fully comprehend until a few years later.

I looked at my watch. The event was almost over, and Matt had still not shown up. As the evening was coming to a close, the master of ceremonies was pointing out certain guests in the room, and Oprah noticed my name on the program. "How would you like a little taste of fame?" she asked. Next thing I knew, I was being introduced by the MC as "sitting in the back of the room ... with *OPRAH* ... John, stand up ... !" Then Oprah started the whole room chanting *"John, John, John!"* and waving their fists in Arsenio Hall fashion. It was a fitting ending—and beginning. My neck still gets red when I think of it.

Just before she left, Oprah said, "St.Augustine—what kind of name is that?"

"One you'll never forget," I replied (quite brilliantly, I thought). A smile, a firm handshake, and she was gone.

Just before I was ready to leave, Matt finally showed up with some story about a missed flight. "How was the dinner?" he asked. I just laughed. The great and powerful Oz had arranged everything flawlessly. "It was fine."

When I arrived home and told Jackie who my dinner partner was, she looked at me as if to say, "Who was buying the shots?" Her skepticism dropped when I received a letter the next week from Gordon declaring, "It was a delight to meet you at the AAD dinner. Consider Deloris, Oprah, and myself as the first members of your fan club, and our mission is to hoot and holler wherever you are introduced." I keep that letter in a safe place.

The day following the dinner, Stedman, Matt, and I, along with our fourth—a gentleman who worked for King World Productions—spent the day on the course. We eventually came in first place—and not because of my efforts. For me, golf is a relaxing day in the outdoors, but Stedman and Matt should be on the pro tour somewhere. The fellow from King World was my partner, and he spent most of his time talking on a cell phone. We hardly spoke for the first 16 holes, and then he finally put the phone away for the last two holes. We chatted back and forth, and as we finished up and headed into the clubhouse for the afterglow, he said the strangest thing. "You know, you should have your own talk show." Yeah, right, a talk show. Who's going to listen to me?

That was three Michigan Association of Broadcasters Awards for Excellence, 8,000 shows, and 5,000 guests ago. As they say, if you want to make God laugh, tell him your plans.

I don't know if I will ever cross paths with Oprah again or even why it's happened twice before, but I do know this: the Yellow Brick Road is *full* of Munchkins who will guide your way and help you find your way back home to who you really are. You may have to endure a little heat from witches, put up with flying monkeys, and even go get the thing you fear most from the people you fear most, but it's a small price to pay to find your way home—and it's closer than you think.

Every time you suppress some part of yourself or allow others to play you small, you are in essence ignoring the owner's manual your creator gave you and destroying your design.

—Oprah Winfrey

You're Off to See the Wizard

Oprah can teach us a lot about being open to the possibility that everything we need to walk the Yellow Brick Road of life is available if we are willing to be present enough to receive it. I could never have arranged a meeting this flawlessly. Think about it. Matt calls and invites me to play golf. I show up at a dinner, and Oprah takes the seat next to me. Matt's plane is delayed. I end up in Stedman's foursome. Some guy from King World (whom I have never heard from again) tells me I should be doing a talk show. Four years later, I am on the air.

This is just one example of the numerous serendipitous events that have moved or affirmed my direction in life. Sometimes, they all line up like guardians of our future to construct a path we did not even know existed. Maybe another word for this is "congruency." At a dinner table, the Yellow Brick Road was being offered to me through a Munchkin (sorry, Oprah) who just happens to be the most famous woman in the world. It was only when I realized that there was more to me than my past, my mistakes, and my faults that there was room made for my higher self.

So the old adage holds true: When the student is ready, the teacher appears. This time, it was Oprah. Next time, it might be a homeless person or the sun breaking through the clouds just when it's needed or some guy's voice on the radio. You never know. The Wizard is an incredibly intelligent system, and it is always talking in ways we can understand if we choose to listen.

Engaging synchronicity in your life is not something you have to put on the daily planner. In fact, you couldn't do it if you tried. It's about expanding your boundaries of belief to include the possibility that the guidance you seek, the messages you need, and the destiny you desire are part of your world—and always have been.

What do you need to do, and who do you need to be, in order to make your journey on the Yellow Brick Road one where dreams come true?

Start at the Beginning

This would seem like a no-brainer, but that's usually the problem. We think *too much* sometimes. We have immense reserves of knowledge at our fingertips but there is a marked difference between *knowing* and *action.* The Yellow Brick Road starts out with the smallest tip of color below Dorothy's feet. It was only after getting caught in a terrible storm after a perceived loss (when Toto was snatched up by Elmira Gulch) that she left one place and landed in another. Where have you been up to this point in your life? Can you see your dreams from where you are, or have too many witches intervened and thrown you off course? Just like Dorothy, you might have to land in a new place to find the path you are seeking. Most of us resist moving forward because, even if we are miserable where we are, at least it's familiar. Heading in a new direction requires change—often due to a *perceived loss* (like Toto), brilliantly disguised as a divorce, job loss, illness, or even the death of someone close to you. It's called a *leap of faith* because you have to jump from one place to another, often without knowing where you will land.

When we were kids, we paid to go on rides that would give us the "thrill of a lifetime." Now, we mostly live *lifetimes with very few thrills.* Take the first step. It's always the hardest.

Admit You're Dorothy

And yes, this even pertains to the men reading this! As a matter of fact, not only are you Dorothy at some point in your life—running away from home so no one can ever take your dog again—but at various times in your walk on the path you have also been the Scarecrow, stuck in a field not of your choosing with a very uncomfortable pole up your *ass-ets* just hoping that becoming smarter would solve all your problems. We have all been Tin Men (yes, even you women), rusted in place by what other people say about us or a grade we failed, or other flotsam not worthy of a tap of the keyboard—not moving for years and seemingly stuck where we have always been because we've forgotten that faith of the heart is the best oil can there is. I can tell you from personal experience that the Cowardly Lion is a close personal friend of mine. I've lost count of the times I puffed up my chest, roared, and chased people smaller than me (not physically, of course) until I got a smack on the snout in one way or another. What goes around comes around. The same goes for Witches—both good and bad—Munchkins, and flying monkeys. We have been and will be them all at some point in our lives.

Find Yourself a Good Pair of Shoes

The ruby red slippers were really cool to look at and served a very important purpose—to keep the Wicked Witch of the West at bay. Now I am not suggesting that you go out and buy a pair (if you can find them), and I don't expect any of the guys reading this to be heading off to a day on the construction site sporting a pair of size 13 sequined flats. But what did those shoes really represent if not *faith*? They are the one thing that Dorothy was told never to lose, for then she would be at the mercy of all the evil the world had to offer. *Faith in yourself* is the one thing only you can develop, claim, and hang onto when every witch seems to be lining you up for a hot meal. The seas of life get rough sometimes, and we all need an anchor. Find one or two things you can hang onto until the storms pass. Use your favorite music or quotes. Read the holy book of your choice, light a candle, or watch *Oprah*—whatever it takes. Just don't take those shoes off, no matter how much Elmira "West Witch" Gulch threatens you.

Fight Fire with Water

From time to time, *they* are going to catch up with you. It could be that you picked an apple or two over the limit, and you got pelted. Or maybe you are minding your own business, and your favorite witch decides to throw a fireball your way or a gang of flying monkeys beats the stuffing out of you. Whatever it is, keep this reminder close by: the reason (with few exceptions) that fire fighters use water to battle the flames are because the two don't mix very well. Water will eventually drown a fire. So when the flames get intense, *don't add oil*—it just spreads the fire in places it doesn't need to be. And *never use a flamethrower* (though it may be tempting) to put out the blaze. People who go around starting fires—whether with a match or with their words—are literally burning themselves in the end. You know who the flammable people are. Stay away from them or you risk the chance of being burned alive. Life is too short to go around putting out fires and being charred all the time.

Are You the Wand or the Wizard?

This, of course, is the age-old question: Who is the real Wizard in all this? As I mentioned earlier in this chapter, I don't remember sitting down and planning out a way to meet up with Oprah on a cruise ship or at dinner. If I had my druthers, I would have skipped getting hit by a drunk driver, and the anxiety attacks that nearly ended my marriage and had my wife and me sleeping on the floor with the lights on for a year, watching *Back to the Future* every night so I could fall asleep—all in order to be on that cruise ship at the right time to meet Ms. O. Now the golf thing was far less painful, but just as incredibly orchestrated. Perhaps when we think we are the Wizard—the one who has all the answers—not much happens, but when we get better at being the wizard's wand—by being receptive to the messages we hear from the Wizard—things get interesting, if not downright magical. Take five minutes and list a few things that have happened in your life that could only be done by the Wizard and not the wand, and you will see the role that synchronicity has played in your life. (Remember: when in doubt, write it out.)

The Yellow Brick Road of life beckons each of us, but unfortunately too many of us ignore its call. By not listening, we miss out on the real magic of being alive. We never get to experience our own Professor Marvel or Glenda the Good Witch or even the Wicked Witch of the West, for without one the others could not exist. We would never dance with the Scarecrow—*that part of us that already knows what to do;* the Tin Man would stay locked deep inside, and *our heart would remain separate from its purpose to light up the world;* and the Lion of Courage would never be heard from *in a world that needs to hear its roar.* And we would never know that the great Wizard of Oz—the all-knowing, all-seeing, all-being (*someone we thought could give us the answers*) is really just a human hiding behind a curtain if we dare to look. Sound familiar?

I don't know where your path will take you—how many witches you will have to fight off or how many broomsticks you might need to find and dispense of. I have no way of knowing if you will ever sit down to dinner with one of the world's most powerful women or win the Nobel Peace Prize or find a cure for some disease. But I do know this: if you dare to step on the path, all manner of help will come your way, and through the most amazing circumstances and people that the Wizard has to offer, they will eventually lead you back home to whom you really are. Perhaps the folk-rock group America said it best: *"Oz never did give nothing to the Tin Man that he didn't already have."* You may not be in Kansas anymore, but so what? Now what? See you in Oz.

CHAPTER 10

Partnership Is Power

You will always move toward anyone who increases you and away from anyone who makes you less.

—Mike Murdock

On a summer night in 1986, I was standing among thousands of others at the UIC Pavilion in downtown Chicago, yelling at the top of my lungs for the hometown boys. A Bulls game . . . ? A rally for the Chicago Cubs . . . ? Naw . . . something *bigger* . . . pro wrestling! Ozzy Osbourne's "Iron Man" began to fill the giant arena. The lights went out, and directly behind me and up on a riser, the spotlights blazed and the announcer's voice permeated the cavernous building. *"Ladies and gentlemen . . . from Chicago, Illinois, at a combined weight of 585 pounds . . . Hawk and Animal . . . the Road Warriors!"*

With their foreboding face paint, weird Mohawk hairdos, and trademark spiked shoulder pads, the Road Warriors were one of the most overwhelming sights in wrestling in the '80s and '90s. Also known as the Legion of Doom, Hawk and Animal used their immense brute strength and incredible agility (not to mention their intimidating presence) to become the most dominating tag team ever to enter the squared circle.

As they had done a thousand other times, they began their walk to the ring and their awaiting opponents. Joe "Animal" Laurinaitis led the way, sporting a Mohawk haircut, his face painted with black around the eyes, and a spider in the middle of his forehead. At 6-foot-2 and tipping the scales at over 300 pounds, he was the more massive and powerful of the two men. He pushed through the crowd with his spiked football shoulder and forearm pads as the fans reached out to touch a legend. Right behind him was the high-flying, volatile, and vocal Michael "Hawk" Hegstrand, a 6-foot-3, 275-pound human missile wrapped in a bodybuilder's physique, with a "reverse" Mohawk and face painted with raptor wings. He also wore the required garb made of leather and steel.

The crowd roared its approval as the two titans dispatched their opponents with a combination of raw strength, agility, and teamwork. As I headed home after the show that night, little did I know what the future held. In less than ten years (a mere blip in cosmic time), I would know how important Joe and Mike would be in my life—and the incredible lessons I would learn from both of them.

Their journey together actually began before they ever entered the wrestling ring. Joe and Mike grew up on the rough side of Chicago. Long before Joe entered the wrestling business, he was an all-American for both football and baseball. Even though he was offered several scholarships for baseball, football was his passion. He was on the NFL radar screen before an injury changed the course of his life. Mike did things a little differently, like collecting gambling debts and being an enforcer—a role that prepared him to become part of the greatest wrestling tag team ever.

Eventually, they both moved to Minneapolis, where they became bouncers in one of the toughest joints in the area called Gramma B's. Since they were already tossing people around, it was a natural transition that Joe and Mike made their way into the world of wrestling. A wrestler named Eddie Sharkey discovered them, and he took them under his wing and trained them. (You might have heard of one of Sharkey's other students: a guy named Jesse "The Governor" Ventura!) No one at that time could predict that two wrestling legends were in the making. Animal and Hawk were born.

In 1983, the Road Warriors made their debut in Georgia Championship Wrestling with their new manager, Precious Paul Ellering, and captured the NWA Tag Team title. It would be the first of countless titles in every major federation—championship belts and awards that the boys would earn over the next 21 years on the road to dominance and a place in the hearts of fans all over the world as the best of all time.

I will leave the rest of the story of the Road Warriors up to Joe when his own book comes out, because this space is reserved for some of the times we spent together. I met Joe while playing in former Minnesota Vikings Matt Blair's Celebrity Golf Tournament. Actually, we met the evening before at Planet Hollywood in Minneapolis. Joe and his wife Julie were hanging out because he was playing in the tournament as well. I had never been formally introduced, even though I had been watching The Road Warriors do their thing on TV (and in stadiums) over the years. I walked over to the table and we talked for a bit, and then we headed out for a steak dinner. I had never seen someone eat so fast! Joe explained that when he and Hawk were on the road, there was little time to waste, and every time I had a meal with these guys it was like having two industrial-strength Hoovers at the table. I know my way around a knife and fork, but these two made me look like a baby in a high chair!

A few weeks later, I met Hawk, and in so many ways we were like the Three Musketeers. The image they portrayed in the ring was in sharp contrast to the men I got to know from so many angles. Joe would fly to Japan, wrestle for a week, come home and, before jet lag could set in, be on the field coaching his son James (who is now a line-backer for Ohio State University) in football or his daughter Jessica (who you will probably see on the Olympic women's ice hockey team someday). The man who can bench-press 500 pounds with ease is one of the most attentive and supportive fathers I have ever met. The big man tears up at the mention of his son Joe Jr., who is a sergeant in the U.S. Army and has served in Iraq. Joe and Julie have created a grounded, loving, and spiritual home for their kids. In so many different ways, he is the brother I never had.

Then there is Hawk. Spending time with Mike was like taking a 6-foot-3, 275-pound kid to Disneyland every single day! The only thing bigger than his shoulders was his heart for people, especially young people. One of my fondest memories of Animal and Hawk was the time I booked them at the Rosemont Horizon in Chicago for the Special Olympics. I had been doing some marketing for the boys, and an opportunity arose for them to participate. The arena was filled with sports stars, but the longest autograph line belonged to the world-famous Road Warriors. Everyone wanted a chance to meet them.

Just before the show, "Uncle Animal" got the idea to paint my kids' faces, so there was 6-year-old Amanda sitting on a chair while Joe duplicated his face paint on her, and over in the corner was 4-year-old Andy being decked out by Mike like "Uncle Hawk." I can still see the smiles on the kids' faces to this day.

I could go on and on with stories about these two, but that's for another time. Both men were in a very unique position, having to rely on each other for not just their professional performance, but also using their partnership to forge a bond that is a model for success in any area of life. *No one succeeds alone.* Like a marriage, no partnership is always smooth and straight. Mike was the more volatile of the pair; Joe was the businessman and leader. Their partnership was tested time and time again over the years. Injuries and the strain that goes with being public figures and being recognized all over the world often took its toll. But in the end, just as in the beginning, the boys grew from being around each other, and in doing so, they became role models for other athletes on how to survive the rigors of life.

I moved to Michigan in 1996, and except for a few phone calls, I lost touch with Joe and Mike. Every now and then, I would see their faces on a wrestling magazine or on television. Joe did my radio show once in 1998, but as with all things, time and paths change. In August 2003, I was in Chicago on business and happened to see that the boys were in town wrestling, but the timing didn't work out and I didn't catch the show. In hindsight, I wish I had made the extra effort. Just a few months later, that decision really haunted me.

On October 20, 2003, I called Joe and left a message. It was a funny thing, really, that I made that call because we had not talked for quite a while. But for some reason it felt really important that I get in touch with him. A few hours later, my wife Jackie told me that Joe had called back and that I needed to come home and call him *right away.* I said I would just call him from my cell phone. *No,* she said, *just come home and listen to the message.* When I heard Joe's voice on the answering machine, my heart sank. Mike had passed away the night before. I was stunned. Mike and his wonderful wife Dale had been in the process of moving into a new home, and around 10:30 that night he felt tired and went to lie down. He never woke up. At the age of 46, one of the most dynamic men I had ever known had made his transition, and it was learned later that a condition called *cardiomyopathy—* a weakening of the heart muscle—was the cause of death. While Mike had battled many demons during his life, the last eight years had been drug- and alcohol-free, and he had become a born-again Christian. While his life may have seemed out of order for long periods of time, at the end—perhaps when it matters most—he was on solid ground and had become the man he had always hoped to be.

Mike's death brought Joe and me back to the friendship we once had. We laughed and cried about the antics of yesterday and the many roads we had traveled. On the day of Mike's memorial, Joe and I stopped to pick up Hawk's cremains from Dale on the way to church. As was his style, Mike was in a Versace bag, and we buckled him in between Julie and Jessica. *"Hawk in a Box"* was the thought of the day. I was doing all right until the eulogies started. I totally lost it, as did everyone else in the church. At one point, Hawk's only other tag partner from Japan remembered how they spent a month together traveling. Neither one spoke the other's language, but it did not matter. Through an interpreter, Kensuke Sasaki said in tears, "Hawk taught me to speak heart to heart."

Joe was the original "Road Warrior" way back when and is now caretaker of the legacy he and Mike created. An astute businessman and entrepreneur, he would be equally effective as a defensive line coach in the NFL or running the marketing department for a major corporation. With his worldwide connections, however, Joe Laurinaitis has the future at his fingertips, due in large part to the *leadership through partnership* he has shown over the years. The man knows how a team works and what it means to put the right people in the right position for the right results.

A lot of changes and lessons can take place in 21 years. For Joe and Mike, it was often a seesaw ride. Countless dates had to be kept. They spent many a night in a rental car, one sleeping while the other drove to the next event. Days and weeks away from home in Japan and

Europe took its toll. The intense spotlight of fame is often like a millstone that can either sharpen you up or grind you down, depending on what angle you take it from.

Mike admitted that he put his body through the wringer, abusing drugs and alcohol as a way to cope with the pressure and fill the emptiness inside that often comes without a strong connection to the real purpose of one's life. Joe, the steadfast partner, pulled Mike back from the brink many times and often feared that one day he would walk into a hotel room to find him a victim of some sort of overdose. When Joe injured his back in the mid-'90s, Mike moved in a different direction, straining the partnership to the breaking point. But somehow, some way, it rebounded, and they even appeared on a WWE Monday Night Raw event just a short time before Mike's death.

This chapter would not be complete without sharing a day that I spent with Joe and Mike in Chicago at the high school I attended and where I later taught. I brought the boys to Schurz High School on the northwest side to speak to various classes about the importance of education. I knew that with their imposing stance and worldwide fame that they could reach kids at a level few others could. The school is like many others in Chicago—a mixture of young people from all backgrounds and ethnicities, sorely in need of someone to remind them that high school is not real life and that the future has room for them if they want it bad enough.

So "Professors" Animal and Hawk were seated in an empty classroom when the buzzer rang. You can only imagine the looks on the students' faces as they filed in, yelling and banging around until they saw who was waiting for them. Then . . . *silence*. The chairs slowly filled up. Hawk didn't wait for an introduction. Wearing all black, from his cowboy boots to the "doo-rag" with skull and crossbones on his head, he got right to it.

"Augie (my nickname) said that there are some real good people that need to be encouraged in this school, and some others that need . . . how do you say it . . . an ass-kicking. Me and my partner Animal are here to give you one or the other. It's your choice."

Hawk started walking around the room, and Animal stood up. With his Mohawk pointing north, he growled, "Hey, listen up! We didn't come all the way here to see you for nothing. We know what it's like to start at the bottom and fight our way to the top. We ain't no different than you, except for one thing. We never quit. Some of you have already given up on yourselves. You think gangs are the way out. Gangs are a dead end, literally."

Hawk jumped back in. "Let me tell you something. Some of you think that you are 'bad' or 'all that.' Until you run into someone who is bigger or stronger—then what? You get whacked. Then because you got whacked, you want to get back at someone. Guess what then? You spend most of your time fighting over nothin' and for nothin' while all the time life is passing your sorry ass by."

He tagged off to Animal, just like in the ring. "Yeah, so here is the deal. In life, there are three types of people: those who make things happen, those who watch things happen, and those who wonder what happened. Now, which one are you going to be?"

Not one kid moved in his or her seat. I think they were too stunned to say anything, but you could see the words were not wasted. Forty minutes later, with the class dismissed, Joe and Mike stood at the door and shook every hand that was offered. They repeated the message six more times that day and never took a dime in payment, just lunch, which they ate in the teachers' cafeteria. When the day was over, the boys had to make their way through the crowd of students and teachers that had converged at the front doors to thank them for coming. It might not have been "Wrestlemania," but it sure changed a few lives that day for the better. Because of the strength of their partnership, Joe and Mike were champions in and out of the wrestling ring. They had leaned on each other for a long time and had a partnership that lasted longer than most marriages. They knew that one of the real secrets to living an uncommon life is this: no one succeeds or fails alone.

The world today is so complex and connected that you will find yourself in partnerships almost by the mere fact that you are alive. How you interact with others is an ongoing partnership, and the lessons you can learn from the greatest tag team in professional wrestling are many. But the lessons you can learn from two life-long friends who traveled the world and became better men because of each other are even more evidence that the right partner doubles your chances of success.

Separately, we are strong, but together we are invincible.
—Michael "Hawk" Hegstrand and Joe "Animal" Laurinaitis

What a Rush!

The world can be harsh, with 6 billion people crawling all over the place, each of us with different values, beliefs, and backgrounds. We all carry personal and generational challenges, mostly unaware of why we do certain things, and we try in vain to break the chains of our past while working so very hard to live in the present. No one can do it alone.

As tough as the world can be, it is also a nurturing place where people are waiting to meet you, help you, and bring out the best in you. There are those who will support your dreams, help create a greater vision, and move you to a higher level of existence than you have ever known—if you allow them into your life. A partnership is one of the most challenging journeys upon which you will ever embark, but it's well worth the trip as long as you are learning along the way. In many ways, a good partnership is like a two-way mirror. Two-way mirrors work *both ways*, and if you get real close and look through, you might just find someone looking back. Any partnership—be it a marriage or tag-team wrestling (sometimes it's the same thing!)—is on one level about working together to reach a goal, but on another level it's about each partner exposing and sometimes compensating for the other's weak points. It's about people putting aside what makes them different and focusing on what they have in common that creates a winning effort.

You can never lose what makes you unique in the world, but you *can* fall short of getting where you would like to go—to the top of the mountain or the top of the charts or even to the pinnacle of sports entertainment—by not recognizing where *you end and someone else begins*. It takes two to tango, and every great achievement always involves more hands, hearts, and hopes than most of us ever realize or admit.

Hawk and Animal took partnership to the extreme in *and* out of the ring. Applying a few moves on your own can help you put a headlock on good partnerships.

Be Honest

You might already have it all, but you didn't *do* it all. Look back and make a list of the people who have contributed to your efforts over the years—even the ones you didn't particularly get along with. (In fact, some people, by way of their very challenging natures, have the most to teach us!) Now take a look at the Acknowledgments page in this book. There is quite a list of names there (the ones I could remember!), but that's just on the surface. Someone designed and printed this book. Someone drove it to the bookstores. Someone at the bookstore put it on the shelves. Someone (like you) bought it. My hands only touched the keyboard, but other hands put it in your hands. Knowing that you are always engaged in partnerships of one kind or another makes every one of them work better. Keep your "acknowledgments list" close at hand and make sure you add to it now and then. Why?

Because *when in doubt, write it out.* This will remind you that the only thing you do by yourself is go to the bathroom (that is, until you really do need help from someone else).

Do What You Know

Without going all "Dr. Phil" on you here, it is important to consider that you don't know everything you need to know to succeed, and, perhaps more importantly, *you don't need to know everything.* I can sit down for three hours and pour my heart and soul into a microphone, which then transmits the vibration of my voice into some sort of sound waves that run through a line somewhere that somehow reaches people in their cars, homes, and offices. My part begins and ends at the flip of the "on-air" switch. Engineer Al, like Engineer Jeff before him, partners with me (whether they like it or not) by making sure that the miles of cables, tubes, and transistors are all doing their thing. I have no clue as to how these guys sit in the middle of what looks like a room full of pasta and sort through and connect all the wires and electrodes, but I do know that they can. Outside of occasional good-natured, on-air harassment, the engineers do their thing, John does his thing, the listeners listen, and we create a result that works.

Partnerships are most effective when each player knows his part and stays out of the others' parts. Sounds simple, but because we are humans and have egos, it bears reminding. Know your part and let others do their part, and you may never have to "part ways."

Tag-Off

Quite often in the beginning of a partnership—or any relationship for that matter—time spent together is at a premium. When you connect with someone who brings something to the table that you don't have, the tendency is to inhale as much as possible. Think back to when you were falling in love and wanted to be on the phone with that person 24/7 and thought of little else. Over time, of course, that changes, but often partners can get too close and spend too much time together, which can cause the opposite effect from what the partnership was designed to create and begin to blur the line of effectiveness. Getting on each other's nerves is a sure sign that you need some adult supervision—apart. If you are in business with a partner, take turns having weekends off and letting the other person (no matter how hard this may be) handle things until you connect again. Turn off (yikes!) the computer and e-mail, and don't answer your cell (except in emergencies—and calling about a lost phone number or a question that can wait does not qualify). Partnerships need some downtime. If you don't take it temporarily, you might hit the mat permanently.

Learn While You Earn

Author Terry Real once said, "We always marry our unfinished business," and the same holds true for other partnerships. Just as partners can bring tremendous talent, connections, and value to the dance, they also bring along their baggage, like it or not. No partnership exists that does not have its struggles. It really has little to do with the job or project, but rather because the weaknesses of each partner are revealed (just as their strengths are) during the process of partnership. Partnership is about learning lessons. We are paired up by the *architect of the universe* with those who can teach the most in ways that may seem difficult on the surface, but absolutely perfect in the big scheme of things.

So many people have the opportunity to learn about themselves by being in partnerships, but they throw it away because the lessons are too hard. Take a deep look at the many partners in your life. Those people are there for a reason, some for a season, and often both. You don't have to know why. It will be shown to you when the time is right—and you are ready.

Be There

Your partners are going to screw up—fall down, lie, get drunk, forget to file the taxes, and, at times, act really stupid. They will get on your every last nerve, talk out of turn at meetings, and make you wonder why you ever agreed to get into business or a marriage together. In short, they will be doing the human thing. Over the years, I watched Hawk and Animal go through tremendous challenges with each other, but the big *ah-hah* is that they were always there for each other, no matter what. Even if a partnership ends, hold on to the possibility that someday, in some way, you may meet again—and remember that all the roads you traveled together had meaning. That in itself is enough to respect the partnership. That does not mean that you go outside the bounds of what you know is right for you, but consider the fact that since partnerships are an integral part of everyday life—and that none of us accomplish anything on our own—someday you might just be knocking on someone's door in need of support, be it cash, a place to sleep, or just an ear to bend. What goes around comes around, and partnerships have a way of bringing out the best and the worst in others and ourselves. But when the need is there, be there to the best of your ability. I assure you that your efforts—whatever they may be—will not be lost in the moment. They will echo in the halls of time and be presented to you when you need them the most. Partnerships are not just about others, but also about who *we* are in relation to our partners and, most importantly, to ourselves. Be there.

CHAPTER **11**

Balance Is Possible

If there was but one word that describes the
most important law in the universe, the word
would be . . . balance.

—Dr. Walter Russell

From Mighty Mite football all the way through high school, college, and semi-pro, football, sports, and athletics have always been a big part of my life. My buddies and I wore out the basketball nets at the park near my home on summer evenings, and for years I played 16-inch softball Chicago-style (the only real softball in my opinion). There are many lessons to be learned from participating in sports that can translate into everyday life, like teamwork, discipline, perseverance, and commitment to a goal. When I was about 10, I used to watch football games on the little black-and-white Sears TV my folks had, and I'd roll up a bunch of socks into a football and dive over the couch to score a touchdown for the Bears in the living room. Those socks remind me of one of the greatest athletes to ever grace the Olympics: Dorothy Hamill. You wouldn't think that a tough-guy jock like me would be impressed by a figure skater, but Dorothy has more stamina and courage in her little skates than many a football player I've known.

Dorothy was born in Chicago, Dorothy's family soon moved to Riverside, Connecticut, and it was there where she borrowed her brother's skates and stuffed some rolled-up socks into the toes to make them fit. Binny Pond was her stage, and all she wanted to do was learn to skate backwards like the other kids on the ice. It did not take long for Dorothy to tap into the energy and talent that would make her a household name. It was on the ice where she felt she could "just be herself." How many young women long for that feeling?

With the encouragement of her parents, Dorothy headed to the rink at 4 A.M. every morning for seven hours of practice, forfeiting the usual teen routine, but with no regrets. As Dorothy's talents grew, she began to work with Gus Lussi in Lake Placid in 1969 and won the National Novice title that same year. After she won the silver medal at the Junior Nationals competition in 1970, the late Carlo Fassi, who was Peggy Fleming's coach when she won an Olympic gold medal in 1968, asked Dorothy to train with him at the Broadmoore Skating Club in Colorado Springs.

An athletic skater, Dorothy feared she'd never be as graceful as Peggy Fleming. Therefore, she resolved to jump better and higher than anyone else. Although she was capable of doing triple jumps, she did not do them in her competitive programs because they weren't considered necessary at the time. In fact, Dorothy was the last female skater to win an Olympic gold medal without triple jumps in her program.

Dorothy also suffered from terrible shyness and, unknown to spectators, was frequently terrified before skating in competition. This nearly led to catastrophe at the 1974 World Championships in Munich, Germany, when Dorothy was just 17. Right before Dorothy skated, Gerti Schanchet, a German skater, performed in front of an appreciative home crowd. When her scores came up lower than expected, her fans began to boo! Gerti stayed on the ice, waving, even after Dorothy's name was called. As Dorothy began to take her place, she was completely unnerved as the crowd continued to boo. Thinking that the crowd was being hostile toward her, Dorothy burst into tears and left the ice. The referee tried to control the audience while Dorothy cried in her father's arms. Planning to leave to compose herself, Dorothy returned to the ice to retrieve her guards, but to her surprise the audience began to cheer when they realized how much they'd hurt her with their booing. She decided to go ahead with her performance, eventually earning the silver medal!

Dorothy won a gold medal at the 1976 Olympics in Innsbruck and became the most sought-after figure skater for commercial endorsements in history. She signed a lucrative contract with the Ice Capades and skated with them for many years. Her other appearances included: *Nutcracker on Ice* with Robin Cousins, a TV version of *Romeo and Juliet on Ice*, a tour with John Curry, a starring role in *Stars on Ice*, and television specials with Andy Williams, Perry Como, and Gene Kelly. After winning the World Professional Skating Championships five years in a row, she was inducted into the U.S. Figure Skating Hall of Fame in 1991. Pretty impressive for a shy little girl who just wanted to skate backwards!

The first time Dorothy was a call-in guest on my radio show, we talked about the challenge of role models and how kids watch every move their heroes make. All it took was the mention of Charles Barkley's comment about not wanting to be someone's role model when I heard a groan on the other end of the line. "It's not a question of whether some young person wants to be like a Barkley, Hamill, or Yamaguchi. The fact is, it comes with the territory. We have athletes who are paid huge sums of money and want all that goes with it—except for the responsibility part of being in the public eye." It was more than refreshing to hear an athlete who had reached the pinnacle of her sport hold the line on accountability.

We spoke about the challenges of being a single parent to her daughter Alexandria, globe-trotting in Third-World countries to help inoculate babies, and what it's like to keep it all together after putting her body through the rigors of training for so many years.

My producer arranged for a ticket to the Champions on Ice event and the opportunity to meet Ms. Hamill in person. I drove to the event (the first time I had ever attended anything on ice except a Chicago Black Hawks game) in anticipation of not only meeting an Olympic champion, but also a woman who was a role model for so many Americans. It was all pretty neat stuff.

The show was more than I could put into words. I was overwhelmed by the strength, precision, and ability displayed by the skaters. Of course, the packed crowd rose to its feet when Dorothy was announced. Her routine brought a hush to the auditorium, and thousands sat in amazement as she carved the ice with her grace and power, ending in a blur with her famous "Hamill Camel" move.

We had time to speak briefly after the show and Dorothy told me to keep in touch. I had a long ride home and kept re-running the evening over in my mind. It was a real eye-opening experience for someone who usually equates sport and ability with pigskins and home runs.

In July 2002, I had the opportunity of a lifetime: to give life to one of my own children for a second time. My daughter Amanda was born with a kidney defect, and she lost her right kidney at the age of 5. By the time she was 13 her remaining kidney was failing. I turned out to be the perfect match. The incredible doctors and staff at University of Wisconsin Children's Hospital did everything just right, and Amanda is now a thriving teenager without any problems.

On my last show before the transplant, my producer notified Ms. Hamill of the impending surgery, and, much to my surprise, I received a call from Dorothy on the air. Near tears, she thanked me for doing what more people should be doing: giving. Her call, along with those of many other guests and listeners, greatly helped in my recovery.

Six months later, I received another call from Dorothy, this time inviting Amanda and me to the Champions on Ice event in Green Bay, just a couple hours from our home. She provided Amanda and me with front-row seats and backstage passes. As the lights dimmed and the music rose, one by one the skaters flew down the ice. Shortly, the rink cleared, the spotlight gleamed at center ice, and in came Dorothy as if on a breeze. After she had finished her routine, Amanda looked at me and simply mouthed the words: WOW!

After the show, we met Dorothy backstage, and the hug she gave Amanda was right from the heart (where the best energy comes from). They talked about sports and parents and how important it is for Amanda to stay healthy after her transplant. It was a great ride home. "You know what, Dad?" Amanda told me. "You have some really cool friends."

But it wasn't until a few months later, when Dorothy appeared on the ABC *50th Anniversary Celebration* with Olympian Carl Lewis, that it really hit Amanda who she had spent time with. "Dad, look, it's Dorothy!" she pointed out. Television always brings home the point.

A couple of months later, I was working on my syndicated one-minute vignette "Powerthoughts!" and the subject was balance. Why not go to the expert? I thought. I called Dorothy, who answered with her usual cheery, "Hey, there!" When I asked Dorothy about her concept of balance and what it meant, she told me, "Balance comes in three parts as it pertains to skating. The first part is when you are up. The second part is when you are falling, and the third is when you hit the ice. Maintaining your balance even though you are going down is really important when it comes to getting up again. You have to make sure you have stopped falling before you get up and get on with the routine." A couple of summers have passed since that conversation, but I have never forgotten her words.

Not too long ago, I had the opportunity to catch up with Dorothy again as she was performing in *Broadway on Ice* with the incredible vocalist Davis Gaines and the musical comic genius of pianist Dale Gonyea. Imagine a full Broadway show complete with a baby grand piano, the booming tenor of Davis, and Dorothy skating on an impossibly small skating surface that looked about the size of half a basketball court. I attended the show with my longtime friend Ginny Weissman and simply stared in amazement for the entire performance. It made her lesson of balance just that much more impressive. It occurred to me that it's not the size of the rink you skate in, but the balance you develop that allows you to skate on the ice of your choice.

First famous for the wedge haircut that started a fashion craze, Dorothy Hamill is now known all over the world, has been voted "The Most Trusted Woman in America," and advocates for many charities and organizations that have touched the lives of millions. She has traveled to Ghana to immunize babies and been named "Headliner of the Year" in Las Vegas, but the most important life she touches is that of her daughter Alexandria. And it's all because she wanted to feel the wind in her face and skate backwards on a small pond as a young girl.

Thirty years have passed since Innsbruck. She battles osteoarthritis, but still laces up her skates six days a week for two hours at a time followed by off-ice training. "After all these years, there is still something to learn from skating every day. And I love it. It's my therapy," she says. She is amazed that people still come to see her perform, but after watching her glide across the frozen surface, I'm not. If a human being can balance on a quarter-inch steel blade while flying across frozen water backwards and defy gravity, what can you do that you have not yet done?

Everybody falls down at one time or another. The key thing to remember is to make sure you have stopped falling before you try to get back up.

—Dorothy Hamill

Applying the Principle of Balance

Teacher and philosopher Dr. Walter Russell wrote that there is one word for the law of the universe and that word is *balance*. And then he said, "If man needs two words to aid him in his knowing of the workings of that law, those two words are: *balanced interchange*." Then he added, "If man still needs more words to aid his knowing of the law, give to him another one, and let those three words be: *rhythmic balanced interchange*." These three words not only define the workings of this incredible system of which you and I are an integral parts, but it also describes the forces that Dorothy Hamill engages to move across the ice on a blade roughly the width of two pennies. And perhaps more importantly, the same concept of which Dr. Russell spoke and that Dorothy has mastered on the ice can be applied to your life—even if you never lace up a pair of skates.

So how does Dorothy Hamill's theory of balance apply to your everyday life? It might help to look at an example. Let's say you've been inspired by the success of the Harry Potter books, and you feel certain you have it in you to be the next J.K. Rowling. For the next three years, you spend every spare minute writing your own Harry Potter novel. Your total focus is on crafting this book because you're certain it's going to be a hit. Finally, you feel it's ready to send to an agent. To your amazement, you begin collecting a string of rejections. "We've seen a million Harry Potter-type manuscripts," they say. "We like your writing, though. What else can you offer?" *What else?* You've just spent three years of your life writing the perfect book. You haven't worked on anything else!

Suddenly, all your years of effort seem wasted. You've taken a very bad fall. Now if, while you were writing the next Harry Potter book, you had also been jotting down other story ideas, studying the market to see what types of books are selling, and honing your skills by writing shorter pieces for magazines or other venues, then the request for other ideas wouldn't have come as such a shock. "The fall" wouldn't have been so painful. You would have dusted yourself off from rejection and offered up other ideas. But you had been so out of balance in pursuing your goal that the fall came swift and fast. And once you "hit the ice," you felt despair.

You had a hard time recovering from the fall. All you could focus on was how you'd wasted three years of your life. You didn't see how you could get back on your feet after taking such a serious blow. If you had spread out your efforts instead, you would have had an easier time rising. After a few days of nursing your wounded ego, you would have gone to your files and pulled out your other ideas. Or you would have taken advantage of the writing classes you'd attended to rewrite your story to fit the current market. But your lack of attention to balance now meant you had to start the "program" all over again. And you just weren't certain you had the energy or the will to do that.

You can see why balance is so very important in pursuing whatever goals you may have, whether they involve writing the next great novel, becoming a figure skater, getting an education, or landing the job of your dreams.

So how can you achieve the same balance that Dorothy Hamill creates to defy gravity and "go for the gold"?

It's doubtful you are going to be attempting any double axels or lutzes in the near future, but you do have to find a way to perform and finish *your* routine every day. Here are a few points to ponder.

Define It

When it comes to maintaining balance in your life, you first have to define it in order to engage and then recognize it. (You may already be doing a good job with balance and don't even know it!) For our purposes, let's define *balance* as a merging of diverse, distinct, or separate elements into a unified whole—or, in other words, *fusion*. I will spare you the physics lesson, but the fact is that every day, in many ways, you are merging diverse or separate elements into a unified whole—or result. When Dorothy does this, she is able to pull the different pieces of her routine into an order that creates a result—usually a standing ovation! When you do achieve balance, it might look like getting the kids to school on time, yourself to work on time, dinner ready on time, and everyone back where they belong on time! Or maybe you have pulled all the different pieces of a project together—the data, information, statistics, and flow charts—that combined give your company a new way of doing business. Once you have defined *balance* in your life, you can accept it and improve on your performance. It's often helpful to keep a one-week journal in which you write down all the things that came together and the results you produced. You might be surprised at how balanced you already are!

Get Out on the Ice

You have to be on the ice to actually ice skate. Humans have primitive nervous systems that took a hit somewhere (I am guessing when reality TV took over!) and we have equated "watching" with "doing"—but they are not the same thing! We love to watch others do what we think is impossible for us, as if the actors, sports heroes, and celebrities of the world are somehow different from us. The truth is, they are not! Most of us have the same equipment, but those who learn to use theirs usually end up skating in front of millions, hitting a home run, or accepting an Oscar. Go rent a pair of ice skates and head out to your local arena. Lace them up and see what you can do! You might fall, but *so what!* At least you are participating in something that improves your balance—not something that knocks you out of balance. Of course, I'm not just talking about ice skating. Go out and start doing whatever you've always dreamed of doing. It may be writing a book, getting an education, or starting a business, but it's never going to happen unless you first "get out on the ice."

Practice, Practice, Practice

I cannot even begin to imagine the countless hours that have gone into Dorothy Hamill's training over the years. When learning to create more balance in your life, you need to come to grips with the fact that you don't start doing triple leaps the first day out. You didn't learn to walk in a week or ride a bike in an hour. It took repetition to learn balance. Most of us take walking or bike riding for granted, but there is a very important lesson there. Once you have mastered something, you don't have to re-create it—just repeat it in whatever area of life you wish to bring more balance, and remember that it's going to take some time. Don't get discouraged. Stay with it until it becomes second nature, whether it is getting to work on time or losing 20 pounds. There is a flame inside all of us. Those who cultivate that fire—feed it, nurture it, and spread it—set the world on fire. It's easy to let that flame get smaller and smaller as the years go by, especially if you have forgotten your particular passion. But the flame is always there. It's your job—and yours alone—to reignite it and see how bright it can become.

Know It's Possible

Just because some area of your life is out of balance now does not mean that it cannot lead to success. Taking a fall doesn't mean you can't get up and try again. People told Roger Bannister that it was impossible to break the four-minute mile, but he did it anyway. Gandhi was told that there was no way he could bring the British Empire down without violence, but he did it anyway. Rosa Parks decided that *enough was enough* and sat down to make a stand that changed America. The list goes on and on. Balance is no different now that you know what it is, where it is, and how you can reach it. Nothing is "impossible" anymore unless you deem it so.

An important factor in creating a life in balance is engaging yourself in something you love to do. Far too many of us settle for less than we can be because we are not willing to put the time, energy, and effort into our dreams. It's a far better existence doing what you love to do, rather than spending a lifetime working for a living because that's all you know. Find people who are doing what you would like to do. Ask them how they got started, what route they took, how they arrived. People who have built their dreams from the ground up are usually more than willing to share what they have learned on the path. They were once where you are and have great respect for the journey.

Put It All Together

This goes back to Dr. Russell and his three very important words: *rhythmic balanced interchange*. What allows a skater to pull off her amazing spins is not some illusion. It's sound principle put into action. A spin combines two forces: centripetal and centrifugal. Skaters engage *centripetal* forces when they pull their arms and legs into the center of their bodies, so in effect they are "pulling themselves together" to achieve pinpoint balance. *Centrifugal* force works in the opposite direction. It's the force that pushes the arms and legs away from the body's core. It's the ongoing balance between these two forces and the skater's position that creates the incredible routines we see on the ice. When a skater pulls himself or herself together—literally—the act of forming "one unit of energy" allows him or her to attain the incredible speed that makes a move possible.

Similarly, *every life has a rhythm to it*. The important thing to remember is that creating an interchange between the coming and going, the rising and falling, the peaks and valleys, is what balance is all about. Your life may appear to be out of balance when in fact it could be that the rhythm of life is changing, and you are right where you are supposed to be. You are learning what you are supposed to learn, and the scales of balance are simply adjusting themselves in your favor. Every event in your life, every situation and challenge, serves a purpose—not to knock you off balance, but rather to help you learn how to improve it. And remember that when you do fall down—and all of us do—make sure that you have stopped your *descent* before you attempt your *ascent*. How do you know when you are ready to get back up? That's easy: you are no longer focused on the *going down*, but rather the *getting up*.

CHAPTER 12

Forgiveness Is a One-Way Street

Forgiveness does not change the past, but it does enlarge the future.

—Paul Boese

opefully by the time you've reached this chapter, you are starting to see a pattern form. While the world seems to be a very strange place indeed, there are people who have cut through the illusion that change is not possible in every aspect of life and left their indelible mark in history by changing their lives. They have, in fact, changed the world. They have developed their talents to the fullest, brought their uniqueness to the world, and have been embraced as leaders, heroes, and icons. But even with all the successes that a person can experience, there is one roadblock to living the uncommon life: our seeming inability to forgive—others *and* ourselves.

There's not a person alive who has not stumbled in some way, shape, or form. Society is quick to "kick you when you're up, kick you when you're down," as Don Henley reminds us in song. Forgiveness is the key that unlocks the door to internal freedom.

Not long ago, I went on an extended road trip, and I thought about all the people I had hurt in my life, intentionally and otherwise.

It occurred to me that while there is so much more to learn about the art of forgiveness, the best place to start was with myself. In order to do that, I had to overlook other people's shortcomings as they have surely overlooked mine. The moment I did that—no matter how "great" or "small" I perceived the situation to be at the time—I let it go. Nevertheless, the process of forgiveness is an ongoing effort. Until we learn these lessons, our journey will continue to be a struggle at every corner we turn.

One of the questions most often asked of me is "Who is your favorite guest?" Personally, I don't think that I could have a "favorite" because each person is so unique that they each fill a niche that only they can occupy. But if I am asked, "What guest has made the most impact on your life?" that answer is easy. It's Jerry Coffee and his lesson about forgiveness.

"When life loses its meaning, when suddenly the world is turned upside down, when there's nothing left that resembles life as we've known it, where do we find the strength and sustenance to go on? For naval aviator Jerry Coffee and others who were held as prisoners of war in North Vietnam, there was only one choice: to go within." That paragraph from the dust sleeve of Jerry Coffee's best-selling book *Beyond Survival: Building on the Hard Times—A POW's Inspiring Story* sets up the journey of a man who experienced seven years of confinement in the Hanoi Hilton. What grabs you most when spending any length of time talking with Jerry is the gentleness in his voice. In a day and age where we spit venom at each other for the smallest infraction, Jerry Coffee's voice is devoid of any bitterness or hatred toward those who did things most humans would have died from, and many did.

Jerry came to the show in 1998 through a good friend, Nancy Vogl, owner of The Universal Speakers Bureau in East Lansing, Michigan. During one of our conversations, Nancy asked me if I had ever heard of a Capt. Gerald Coffee. I told her no. Then she made one of the most accurate statements I have ever heard: "Once you hear Jerry Coffee speak, you will never be the same again." Nancy was right on target.

Born in Modesto, California, Gerald (Jerry) Coffee joined the Navy in 1957 after graduating from UCLA with a degree in Commercial Art. In 1962, during the Cuban Missile Crisis as an F-8 Crusader pilot, Jerry was awarded the Distinguished Flying Cross for flying low-level reconnaissance missions over Cuba, taking the photos ultimately used by the United States U.N. ambassador to prove the existence of Soviet missiles there. In February 1966, while flying combat missions over North Vietnam, his RA5-C reconnaissance jet was downed by enemy fire. He parachuted safely, but was captured immediately. For the next seven years, he was held as a POW in the Communist prisons of North Vietnam. After his repatriation in February 1973, Jerry returned to operational duties and eventually retired from active duty in the Navy after 28 years of service.

On the first show on which Jerry was a guest, he recounted a story so powerful that I totally skipped any commercial breaks and went nearly the full hour straight. He shared his experience of torture at the hands of his Vietnamese captors and the life-changing lessons that came with the most challenging days of his life.

After being shot from the sky and enduring many days of captivity, it was only a matter of time before he was interrogated. Like all POWs, Jerry was trained to resist giving any information that could enable the enemy. Of course, this is easier said than done.

"I sat in front of a man who called himself the 'province administrator.' We were in a room filled with varying levels of military types. The two guards assigned to me stood on each side as the interrogator began to demand information from me on what type of aircraft I flew, what mission I was on, and what ship we launched from. I responded as I was trained to: 'Under the Geneva Convention on the treatment of prisoners of war, I am required to tell you only my name, rank, and serial number, and date of birth. I am Lieutenant Gerald Coffee, 625308, June 2, 1934.'

"'I know who you are,' said the interrogator. I was concerned about my crewman, Bob Hanson, who had ejected with me from the plane when we got hit. One of the guards flashed Bob's military ID card in front of my face. 'He has been shot,' the chain-smoking interrogator said. 'Now what kind of plane were you flying?' He ground his cigarette into the table for effect. I resisted giving any information. 'I have nothing more to say,' I said.

"With that, the guards grabbed me from my chair and hauled me out to the yard and toward a tree where they proceeded to push me back against the trunk. They pulled my arms behind the tree where they tied my wrists together. I was being readied for a firing squad.

"The interrogator walked up to me, looked me in the eyes, and motioned a priest over to me. 'This is your last chance,' he said. 'If you have anything to say to this man of God, now is the time.' The only thing that kept running through my mind was survival training school and the words of the instructor. 'They probably won't kill you because you are something of value to them.' I hoped he was right. There were five rifles pointed at me, and there was nothing I could do about it. The command to fire was given, and one shot rang out from some kid with an old M-1 rifle. The slug came at me in slow motion and buried itself in the tree next to my ear. I waited for more shots, but nothing. However, chaos had broken out. It was obvious from the shouting that something had gone wrong: *No one was supposed to have live ammo!* The whole thing was a setup to break me down, but the kid who fired must not have gotten the message. But I wasn't out of the woods quite yet.

"I was dragged to the other side of the yard, and one of the guards tied a rope around my arms that cut off my circulation. Then with his foot behind my neck and my face down in the dirt, he pulled my arms up behind my head so hard that I could feel the cartilage in my shoulders and sternum giving way. Then they pulled the other end of the rope over a low limb on a nearby tree and proceeded to hoist me up, with my arms bent behind me, until I was in a semi-hanging position. I managed to hold out for a while, but the interrogator grew impatient. The guards decided to take my torture to the next level by pushing me so that my feet could not touch the ground. The pain in my shoulders and arms was unbearable, and I cried out for God. Then they proceeded to take the dirty rag that was my blindfold and stuff it in my mouth—with the barrel of a gun—and did it so hard it cracked one of my teeth. My thoughts about the military code of conduct drifted in between waves of pain. I tried to keep my mind together while my body was being pulled apart. After what seemed like an eternity, the interrogator stood in front of me. 'I was on the Kitty Hawk and flew an RA-5C aircraft,' I whispered. I had done the unthinkable, and it was unforgivable: I had given information to the enemy.

"With that information, they promptly untied me from the tree, and I was led back to the little hut I was confined to. I was given some water and a bowl of soup, but I could not eat. I was ashamed of myself for not having stuck to just my name, rank, and serial number. I tried to rationalize that the information I gave them was meaningless, but I broke just the same. I felt weak, useless, and small, and at some point every preconceived notion I had about victory and defeat was let go."

Just for a moment, attempt to put yourself in Jerry's sandals. Imagine being removed from everything you know, tied to a tree, and narrowly escaping execution, but then being tortured the better part of the day in the blazing sun, with your arms tied behind your back and up so high that the pain makes you pass out. All because someone wants some information that you refuse to give out. Your training is being tested not in a class, but at the hands of your enemy. You finally break and feel the most shame you have ever experienced in your life. You are alone. How would you handle it? How would you forgive yourself? Could you?

Some of the stories that Jerry has shared on air have made me laugh; some have made me cry; all have made me think. How is it possible that he endured years of captivity, all the untold humiliation and terror that goes with it and the thousands of hours alone, at times his only communication a tapping code on the wall of his cell, and yet see his imprisonment as a time of learning when he could easily have become a victim?

"John," he told me, "I have learned a great many things that would have gone unlearned or unnoticed had my life been different. And I like the way my life has turned out. So often we dismiss a teaching because of the way that it is taught. So often we deny ourselves great moments because the moments don't look so great when we are in them. Forgiveness is essential to learning and growth. Forgiveness does not condone what happened to you or those who did it to you, but rather forgiveness breaks the chain that keeps you dragging the situation into moments where it does not belong. If I did not forgive those men for what they did, I would still be in prison to this day in the place where true freedom exists—in my mind. The only option for change and forgiveness is to go within."

All this coming from a man who was beaten and tortured, both physically and mentally, at the hands of fellow human beings. What, then, is the key to freedom from this kind of oppression, hatred, and pain? The same thing that will open the doors to a better tomorrow, no matter what has transpired in your life—forgiveness.

Just confining Jerry Coffee to the lesson of forgiveness is really selling him short. Wrapped up in his incredible journey is the will to live when there seems to be no way out. The faith that became his guiding light in the North Vietnam darkness illuminates his life and those of anyone who comes into his flight pattern. Despite being a highly decorated hero, he is a humble man. He sees and understands the good fortune that has come his way as a by-product of sharing his story with people from all walks of life. The deeply rooted patriotism he exemplifies is at the heart of his very existence.

We live in times that demand forgiveness—of ourselves first and foremost—for the venom that is spewed between political parties, the gossip that consumes us, the untruths the talking heads of the media create, and the seeming inability of many Americans to follow the words of our own Pledge of Allegiance: *"One nation . . . indivisible, with liberty and justice for all."*

Captain Jerry Coffee has gone beyond *surviving* to *thriving* because he mastered the most difficult mission that any of us can ever undertake—forgiving ourselves. There is a lot we need to forgive—playing small, not stepping up to the next level, not making a change and a difference, and for not being better stewards of our world on our watch. After enduring seven years of horrible, senseless torture, Jerry returned home a better human being. So what possible reasons could you have for not doing the same?

The decisions we make out of loneliness and pain, uncertainty and fear can take us to the extremes of shame and pride. The turning point that changes adversity into opportunity, defeat into victory comes when we are willing to forgive ourselves.

Too often unreasonable expectations lead to self-judgment and guilt.

—Capt. Jerry Coffee, USN (Ret.)

Forgiveness Is Freedom

Forgiveness carries with it so many definitions and applications that perhaps there are too many options to choose from, so we don't forgive at all. It's like standing in the deodorant aisle and trying to pick how you want to smell when you sweat: they all do the same thing, but making the choice is the hardest part. At the heart of every religion is the concept of forgiveness—the power it contains and the freedom that comes with it. But neither the power nor the freedom can be accessed unless we begin with forgiving ourselves.

It's been said that there are two major sins in the world: the sin of commission and the sin of omission. According to St. Thomas, the sin of omission was about leaving out the good, which is less grievous than a sin of commission, which involves a positive taking up with evil. Without going into a theological debate over what constitutes evil and sin these days, maybe this example works better. You are driving down the street and a little old lady is crossing. You speed up to make the light and clip her just enough to send her to the pavement. That's the sin of commission. You made a choice, given all the facts at the moment, to take the action that results in a consequence. The sin of omission is what happens when you keep driving after you hit her and leave her next to the curb. That's even worse—you could have done something to alleviate the pain you caused—but *chose* not to.

Forgiveness works the same way. Not one of the 70 billion humans who have walked the planet since the beginning of time has been exempt from making a miscalculation in judgment—either on a worldwide scale or in the privacy of their own lives. It's a fact of life that we are going to fall down over and over again. But going back and picking up the pieces are essential to moving forward in life. One "crutch" that can help us rise to our feet again is forgiving ourselves. It is in the rising that the real power of forgiveness is revealed.

Jerry Coffee spent over 2,500 days imprisoned in a dank, filthy, rat-infested cell. He was tortured in the most despicable ways imaginable by other human beings. Every sense of his outer personality was stripped away, and many times death was a reality. And he went on to forgive not only himself for breaking under the pressure, but also the very people who tried to cancel his return trip home as well. Now, who are you mad at? And for what?

Grow Up

We are creatures of emotion. Our primitive nervous system is constantly demanding that we respond to outer stimulation of every kind. It doesn't take much to get people ticked off these days—someone takes "your" parking spot or crosses into "your" lane or ruins "your" life—but everything really comes down to perception. Jean-Michel Cousteau always reminds me that humans are the new kids on the block—teenagers in the big scheme of things—and so often we act accordingly, no matter what our biological age may be. Like adolescents, we are enamored with our toys, we don't like to share, and we forge life-long grudges against those who we perceive to be different from us. Here is a news flash: they *are* different from you. That's how it's supposed to be! Relationships on any level and of every kind are merely opportunities to grow, and in order to grow you have to see the situations of your life as part of an ongoing class in evolution. It's nearly impossible to become all you can be if withholding forgiveness for every small infraction or a penchant for majoring in minor things is your standard operating procedure.

Choose Not to Lose

I was at my father's bedside on a bright May morning when he took his last breath on Earth, just shy of his 70th birthday. We had spent a good bit of time together the last year of his life, but had lost a lot more over the years. Like many sons, I felt for a long time that somehow my father should have been different than he was—taller, richer, funnier, whatever. I somehow just couldn't forgive him for not being who I *thought he should be*. My stubbornness built a gap that was nearly impossible for him to reach across, no matter how hard he tried. In the end, I learned a valuable lesson about accepting people for who they are. When you do that, there is really nothing to forgive—except yourself, for being someone who judges others. Not a day goes by when I wish I could roll back the universal clock and spend time with him—show some courage, take the first step, make the call, write the letter, hold the hand, say what needs to be said. Make a choice to forgive. Time may not be on your side. Do you want to be right or do you want to be happy?

Bless Your Mess

Worry is like chewing gum—it's something to do, but it really doesn't get you anywhere. Worrying about your past mistakes and regrets blocks your ability to forgive and move forward. The human mind cannot consider two opposing thoughts at the same time. It does not know past from present or future; it only acts on what it "sees." Take some time to make a list of your mistakes, screw-ups, lies, and sins—whatever vernacular works for you—big and small. Only you know what you need to "for-*give*" so you can "for-*get*."

Just as there seems to be no order to miracles, there is no order to the things that can be forgiven. Getting right with yourself and "blessing the mess" you have created will help you see your journey in a new, more empowering light. Write it all down, then burn it, share it, or keep it for those days when you think forgiving yourself is out of reach. We have all made a mess of things at one time or another. That's what mistakes are for—to learn how *not* to do something. You might get the lesson the first time around or repeat it for 50 years. Either way, forgiveness is key to locking out yesterday and opening the door to the next moment.

Commute Your Sentence

I hate to be the one to rain on your parade, but you are going to die. Don't worry, so am I, as well as your sports heroes, actors, teachers, parents, and friends. We all are living under a *death sentence*, BUT you can convert your time to a *life sentence* by understanding and practicing forgiveness.

Jerry Coffee has told me numerous times that all of us are imprisoned to the extent of our ability to forgive. Someone could have slighted us 40 years ago, but because we carry that memory, we are shackled to it. Forgiving that person—silently in prayer if you like or in person even if you don't like it—frees you from the *chain of pain* that forges a new link every moment we don't cut ourselves from the past. Capt. Coffee would still be in the most horrible prison there is—the one inside his head, as are so many people for lesser offenses—if he had not summoned the strength to forgive his captors and himself.

Forgiveness Is Free

Holding on to pain will cost you big time. To err is human . . . *to forgive is absolutely necessary* if you want to live an uncommon life. There is a big payoff in being "the victim." People pay attention to you, *but for all the wrong reasons.* There is also a big pay-off in being "the victor." Then people not only pay attention to you, but when you forgive what was and move on to what can be, they gain perspective on their own journey from observing you take yours. My hope is that by reading a little about Jerry Coffee's ordeal, you will be less inclined to condemn the people in your life for every infraction that you deem to be devastating—and even the ones that really are. Forgiveness, like everything else, begins and ends with you. Forgiving yourself takes practice. It has to become a habit. And with all the bad habits humans have garnered over the centuries, it's a good one you should consider developing to its full potential. Forgiving others in no way condones, validates, or excuses their actions or behaviors, but it does reverse the flow of power from them back to you, where it belongs and can do the most good. Let POW in your life stand for: power over weakness—*not* prisoner of woe.

Chapter 13

Go Within or
Go Without

*I know of no more encouraging fact than the
unquestionable ability of man to elevate his life
by conscious endeavor.*

—Henry David Thoreau

ecause we tend to think that history started on the day of our birth, a little perspective is in order at this point. As I write these words, it is Spring 2006, but let's skip back a few years— 101 sounds about right—to the year 1905. Here is a small taste of life before most of us living today were even thought of. The average American male could expect to reach the ripe old age of 46. Women lived slightly longer, to 47. If you were African-American, your life expectancy was 33. Roughly 76 million people were living in 46 states, and 8,000 autos bounced along and occasionally shared the 144 miles of paved roads. There was about $46 million in the U.S. Treasury, and the average worker made nearly $13 for a 59-hour workweek. Children as young as 5 labored in filthy conditions for pennies. Women were arrested for smoking in public—and forget about voting or running for office. Only 14 percent of the homes in the United States had a bathtub, and only 8 percent had a telephone. The five leading causes of death in the United States were pneumonia/influenza, tuberculosis, diarrhea, heart disease, and stroke. There were no depression support groups; no Judge Judy; and no Prozac, Viagra, or Rogaine.

Ahhh . . . the good, old days.

A century is a blink of the cosmic eye, and a few things have changed since then. We have added nearly 30 years to the life span (now at 77.6 years). Our population has swelled to nearly 300 million in 50 states, and an estimated 65 million autos now clog thousands of miles of highways and byways. Forget what's in the Treasury—in 2000, the Texas Rangers baseball team signed shortstop Alex Rodriguez to a 7-year contract worth $252 million—nearly five and a half times the amount the entire country had on hand in 1905. (Of course, he now plays for the Yankees for $25 milion a year.) The average income is around $45,000 per year, and 65-hour workweeks are not uncommon. Child labor laws ended domestic sweatshops, and now the big debate is "smoke-free" rather than "light up, baby." Forget bathtubs—we now have showers with six nozzles on them. There are millions of telephones (in fact, nearly 45 percent of Americans say that their cell phone is their main contact to the world), not to mention really cool ring tones, text messages, and movies on demand right in the palm of our hands. The leading causes of death in 2006 are heart attack, cancer, stroke, emphysema, and accidents—which were barely on the radar screen way back when. We are living a longer, richer, and more technically advanced life than any other humans have ever enjoyed—and yet we are more depressed, stressed, and misunderstood than ever before. Somehow, having it all doesn't translate into being happy. Nevertheless, we do our best to stuff down all the latest trends, fads, and "bling" to give ourselves some sense of identity.

We come into the world with nothing but ourselves, leave with nothing but ourselves, but for some reason, we think that in between we have to be anything *but* ourselves. This is absolutely amazing.

We are stressed out, overworked, underpaid, sleep-deprived, caffeine-driven, and addicted to our Blackberry (not the kind you serve with cream). I am not sure exactly how far we have to go down before we begin to look up, but I know someone who does—Dr. Kathleen Hall.

Whenever a story starts out with "She had it all . . . ," you know two things immediately: you will see yourself in the story at some point, and this is serious, life-changing stuff.

If you were to peek into the upper floors of a New York office building in the '80s in a corner office, which often smacks of success, you might have caught a glimpse of a woman who was dressed for success. She showed all the trappings of achievement—commuting from Atlanta to New York for her career, a fabulous home, incredible vacations, a beautiful wardrobe, brand-new cars, and a sculpted physique. This was Kathleen Hall.

Her carefully planned life—devoid of happiness, but filled with activity—was abruptly sent in a new direction one morning when she stepped into the elevator of the World Trade Center. Kathleen had been following her usual jet-setting routine—grabbing a cab to the WTC and packing herself in the elevator along with the other humans on her way to the 104th floor—but when the door opened, so did her inner self. She experienced a panic attack so severe that it felt like a heart attack, and Kathleen ended up leaning on a wall for three hours until a security guard pried her loose. A week later, she stumbled across the writings of Henry David Thoreau and one sentence in particular leapt forward: *"I went to the woods because I wished to live deliberately, to front only the essential facts of life, and see if I could not learn what it had to teach, and not, when I came to die, discover that I had not lived."* Within a short period of time, Kathleen extracted herself from the high life, cashed in her equity, and went back to the woods to confront her fears and find her faith.

The inward search became an outward path, involving years of study with some of the most revered leaders and sages of our time. She studied with everyone from His Holiness the Dalai Lama to Dr. Thomas Keating to Arun Gandhi, grandson of Mahatma Gandhi, as well as a long line of scientists, priests, nuns, shamans, and former presidents. The one-time Wall Street woman with a degree in finance now held a master's in divinity from Emory University and a doctorate in spirituality from Columbia Theological Seminary, and had gained clinical training from Harvard University. Luxury vacations were replaced by long days working with marginalized children or "throw-away kids" in housing projects. Power lunches were exchanged for time spent giving comfort to homeless women and children in Atlanta. Climbing to the top now meant sitting bedside as cancer and AIDS patients made their transition.

Her life had gone from one of inconsequence, as suggested by a friend, to an existence filled with meaning and hope. She had left the empty path of *upward and onward,* and made a critical, conscious choice to go *inward and downward,* toward the roots of happiness.

Our paths crossed not too long ago, but from the first moments we spoke off-air, and then throughout the show and for quite a while after the program, I knew this was a formidable human being. I understood the language she used: the words of a seeker are colored with experience, tempered with confidence, and are quickly recognized by others who have taken the journey within. The path is different for each of us, but the lessons are always the same.

Our on-air conversation began with an assessment of something I like to call HCI, or Human Confidence Index. I said, "I am convinced beyond a reasonable doubt that we are slowly scaring ourselves into early extinction. First, it was the plague. Then the flu pandemic of 1918. Then it was swine flu. Then Legionnaires' disease. Then SARS, and now it's avian bird flu, which has caused just over 100 deaths in eight years compared with the 350 people who die *each day* in car accidents. Kathleen, what is happening to us?"

"The truth is that a lot of us are living hollow lives. We claim to have great faith, and yet when it comes to really living it, we often choose to accept the view of the world the media presents to us. Fear is the greatest threat to humanity. There is always something out there to get you in here, be it terrorists, global warming, shark attacks, the bogeyman, you name it. We obsess over our children's safety and our waistlines and our credit scores. We need to stop and get a grip. We have lost our trust and, more importantly, our confidence. Think of what the word 'confidence' means in Latin. The word *con* means *with* and *fides* means *faith.* We have lost trust in ourselves. Think back to your grandparents or spend time around true holy people. They have this amazing rooted trust in who they are. We have replaced inner trust with outer things, and the combination has not only made us weaker, but also very unhappy."

"Kathleen, so what you're saying is that it's OK to have things, but when the things have you, there's a problem?"

"Exactly. It's the big lie. We keep coming up with more and more stuff and less and less of ourselves. With all the supposed awareness in the world, you would think by now we would get it. Things don't make you happy. It's just stuff."

"Yep, bottom line is that we are all estate sales in the making. Some of us will just have more tables to set up than others." I could not resist adding that little tidbit. "So what else is connected to the rampant unhappiness?"

"Well, John, another big one is that we make the mistake of identifying who we are with what we do."

"How so?" I asked (knowing full well the answer).

"Well, if you confuse who you are with what you do, then if you stop doing it, you think you're nobody. And with the way the job market is today, the last thing you want to do is think that you are your job," she said.

"Any other contributors to the unhappiness movement?"

"There really is a laundry list, but leisure comes to mind. As a professor who has taught early religion, I can tell you that leisure was designed as a time to stop and bring people together, regardless of their economic station in life. It was a leveling and introspective time. Contrast that concept with the fact the 57 percent of Americans don't take their allotted vacations! We are turning vacation days back in for money to buy more stuff that doesn't make us any happier because we have no time to enjoy anything! The truth is, we don't know how to stop. One of the biggest things for which I am sought after as a media expert is technology stress. The people I deal with cannot turn off their e-mail, even at four in the morning! There is a new code in insurance books for people who overuse their Blackberries because their thumb joint is falling apart. We are chasing technology down a very long black hole."

"OK, so we acknowledge that sometimes—actually, more often than not—humans tend to ... how do I say it ... make a mess of things. What's the answer?"

"I have spent time with some of the greatest pioneering medical minds in the world, and what we found out is that there are four quadrants that have to be addressed for change to take place. I converted these quadrants into something I call SELF-care. S stands for serenity, which is the opposite of stress. We know that if people get quiet for just a few minutes during the day, it makes all the difference in how they feel. Just by invoking a small prayer or mantra, the body relaxes and actually produces endorphins and serotonin, two natural chemicals that actually calm you down. E stands for exercise, but don't confuse it with the 'diet and exercise' treadmill to nowhere. Our bodies were meant to move. Think of your grandparents out chopping wood or working in the garden. These days our biggest activity is walking back and forth to the fridge and trying to find the remote. We have become couch potatoes. The average American spends 90 minutes in a car each day. In order for the body to become holy, it needs to be whole, and movement is the key. *L* is for love. There are many things that give us the opportunity to express and receive love—time with pets, time with friends, time with family, intimate time with your significant other. And we need community, so share your life with someone else. Self-love is self-respect, and since you cannot give what you do not have, increasing the ways you love yourself is critical to being able to receive love. And, finally, *F* stands for food. Do you know that in the last hundred years we have become the first culture to not use food as medicine—for healing and vitality? We want to lose weight so we skip breakfast, not knowing that by eating in the morning, it actually increases the metabolism by 20 percent or more. It's simple things like making sure we get enough omega-3 fatty acids to offset the incredible amount of junk food we take in. The human body is an incredible machine, and it needs to be treated as one. So if you take everything I just said and put it together as SELF, then happiness is a natural result of these four quadrants being in balance as they were meant to be. Make sense?"

Common sense, not common practice.

The natural state of a human is joy. Just look at any infant. Long before someone ever tells him that he comes from the wrong side of the tracks or that he should belong to a particular political party or root for a particular team or do a certain thing for a living, he experiences nothing but pure joy at being alive. Yet he has nothing except his connection to his caregivers and surroundings. Inside each of us is that flame of happiness that has been slowly snuffed out in the process of growing up. As Dr. Kathleen Hall so aptly notes, constantly moving *upward and forward* takes us away from the roots of happiness and who we are, causing imbalance. Conversely, moving *inward and downward* takes us back to what's important and reconnects us to our roots.

One of Kathleen's totems is the oak tree. In fact, her internationally known stress institute in Georgia is called Oak Haven, and with good reason. A giant oak attains tremendous height and strength in its upward growth, but it can do so only because its roots are so deep in the ground. The lesson of happiness as an inside job is always being taught by life. It's just that sometimes we need someone to facilitate the program now and then. Dr. Kathleen Hall heard the voice of greatness calling her from within and was courageous enough to answer. She gave it all up to go back to the bosom of nature and find out who she really is, and in doing so proved once again that circumstances never define the person. They merely reveal the person for who he or she is.

You might consider doing the same as Kathleen. After all, the clock is running and the seasons will not stop coming, but you can fill the remainder of your days with happiness, hope, and harmony, as it was designed to be.

Most of us are living an insufficient life. We are going through the motions, but the motions aren't making us any happier. Living a life of intention is about putting down deep roots of faith, service, honesty, and commitment to a cause larger than us. Happiness is the natural result.

—Dr. Kathleen Hall

Don't Worry . . . Be Happy

I could say that the formula for unhappiness is a no-brainer, but that would be technically incorrect, because the brain is just an organ—like your liver. It's our minds and how we use them that's the problem. If we don't use our mind power in a way that expands our path toward happiness and we *think* we are happy because of who we know, what we do, and what we have then we are setting ourselves up for even more unhappiness—because there is never enough money or houses or cars or drugs or *you name it*. I am amazed that in the 21st century so many people still think that things define who you are—and will "make" you happy.

When I left Chicago in 1996 and put all my stuff—the things I thought defined me—in storage for a year and lived in two rooms at a motel with my family, I got really clear really quick on not only what's important, but also what contributes to happiness. Not surprisingly, it was none of the "things" I was paying to keep locked up in a metal building. The walk to Chicago and back north, and that year in the motel, put me in touch with places within I had not remembered for a very long time. It tested my marriage on levels that could result in only one of two outcomes—stay or leave. (Fortunately, we chose the former.) It taught my children, who were 7 and 5 at the time, the meaning of family, trust, friendship, and a dozen other lessons they never would have been exposed to. A radio friend told me a few years later how much she envied my life. "What an incredible gift to be out of the chaos and living so close to the Great Mystery."

Happiness—contrary to what Madison Avenue and others insist can be found in everything from watches to beer to underwear to new tires—often gets confused with pleasure. Things can give you pleasure, but true happiness is an inside job.

Thanks and a tip of the reggae hat to Bob Marley for putting the above words into a song, and to Bobby McFerrin, who put it on the lips of people all over the world. Worry is like a rocking chair. It doesn't get you very far and certainly doesn't contribute to being happy, but following Dr. Kathleen Hall's lead will.

Run for Your Life!

You know, every hoofed mammal we make part of our food chain thinks that it's got it made—room to graze, plenty of food, and water—with no clue of what awaits it at the end of the line. One by one, they are led to their final destination. In all the years of domesticated animals feeding humanity, you would think that one of them would be smart enough to figure out what was going on. But the humans consuming them often aren't any smarter—mooing away in the pasture, chewing on the cud of life, content with the routine. Everything looks good by all outward appearances, and then one day they're off to the slaughterhouse. It could be a heart attack or stroke or, God forbid, the dreaded thumb joint malfunction from overuse of Blackberry devices. Get out of the pasture while you still have time, even if it's only temporary at first. Get out of the city; climb a tree; lie down in the grass; spend some time (without your cell phone) near a large body of water and just stop for at least 30 minutes. It will take 15 minutes to let the stress of the day drain off and another 15 to fill up your burned-out senses.

Your Money *and* Your Life

You might not be able to "have it all" (at least not all at once), but who said you can't have the best of both worlds—peace *and* prosperity? Too often we are fearful of giving up one thing for another. We think that somehow the universe will not live up to its promise and will leave a void. I am living proof that it's possible. What I gave up by leaving the city was small in comparison with what I was given by living where I do. All the great events of my life were waiting at the end of that walk and I would never have found them if I had not journeyed forth. Are there days I miss Chicago? You bet. Then I order a Lou Malnati's pizza on-line and watch the Cubs on TV or make time to go there for the weekend. There was a living for me to claim—different, for sure, from the one I was used to, but I am so much richer in so many ways. Kathleen Hall had it all, but she decided to listen to the beckoning of her soul. She gave it all up, called in her chips, and began a new life. Now she's known all over the world for her work on stress relief. She went from WTC to CNN because she knew that life is about this *and* that—not this *or* that. So what do you want to be when you grow up? First, you have to go inward and downward to find out.

Survivor—Your Life

I figure, since we seem to be so hooked on TV shows that feature hand-picked contestants in skimpy outfits snuffing out each other's torches on remote, exotic islands, that a good "challenge" is to pretend, for as long as it takes, that you are a contestant. But instead of being on the remote island of *Watchme-Watchme*, your life is the field of play, and the objective is a little different from the show. The only person you are in competition with is yourself. Your mission, should you choose to accept it, is to first realize that even if you win the rat race . . . you're still a rat! Even if you think you have it all, someone will always have more than you. Does that make you less of a person and that some-one more of a person? Slowly begin stripping—not your clothes, but your connections to the devices and things that keep you on virtual life support. Take a real dare and don't answer your e-mail for at least 15 seconds after it arrives. If you need to put on some type of coconut apparel, that's up to you. Bottom line is, in order to go from surviving to thriving, you have to remove yourself from the stimuli that cause the mind to be in survival mode—like riding a metal bullet every day for years on end to the corner office on the 104th floor. You may not want to abdicate your life to the degree that Dr. Hall did, but at the very least carve out time to connect with the best parts of who you are. Keep a journal in your desk that has images of your favorite people and places, and frequently put your thoughts on paper. Take a five-minute mental vacation. Just head off to the island of your choice and return when you are good . . . and ready.

Water Your Roots

There isn't a plant on Earth that can survive without taking water in through its root system. Over millions of years, every type of grounded growing thing, from lichen to cactus to the mighty oak, has nourished itself from within. Each has a unique root system that works best for the environment it inhabits. Some have surface roots that draw water near the topsoil; others send their roots as deep as possible to withstand the winds of change. Either way, both can teach us a very valuable lesson. If you don't have anything that anchors and feeds you, your life span is going to be fairly short. Kathleen Hall defined the four sides of SELF earlier in this chapter. I suggest you find ways to expand on them and make them your own. The roots of true happiness have to be nurtured on an ongoing basis. If they are forgotten, other things take their place, like depression, anxiety, fear, anger, worry, and illness. Katherine Hepburn was once asked that now famous question by Barbara Walters,

"If you were a tree, what kind would you be?" The press had a field day and the late-night guys had their jokes, but Miss Hepburn's answer was important to the person it mattered to most ... herself. "An oak tree," was her reply. So if you want to make a list of what kinds of tree you are most like, have at it. Far be it from me or anyone else to decide what works best for you. For many years, I have kept rhinos around the house—not real ones, of course (the cat wouldn't like it), but rhino pictures, hand-carved key chains, and desk-sized rhinos, most of them courtesy of my friend Scott Alexander, author of *Rhinoceros Success*. The rhino reminds me to stay alert, keep charging, and never give up, no matter what might stand in the way. Keep reminders around that serve to nourish your roots—and only you know what they may be.

Give Yourself to the World

Being unhappy about life is a direct result of disconnect from life. While it's true that watching the news too much will make you more than a little apprehensive about coming out of the house, it's also true that the route to being happy is to give some of yourself to others in need. Kathleen Hall had her life in order—big job, big office, big car, and big house—but very little in the way of service to humanity. She leapt off the bridge of security and now has a "big life" because she gives of herself in such a big way. If you are unhappy with your lot in life, head down to your local homeless shelter and see if there is anyone you might want to change places with. If the aches and pains have caught up with you and put you in a foul mood, head over to the nearest VA hospital for some sympathy. If your happiness is on the decline because of the nocturnal wanderings of some political candidate, make a call over to Turkmenistan or Uzbekistan or Kazakhstan and see how things are going lately. Happiness is all about perspective. And who is in charge of perspective? Anyone? ... Anyone?

At times, being unhappy is a natural response to a situation or condition, but when temporary situations create permanent feelings then, *Houston, we have a problem*. There are hundreds of reasons to be happy. And you know what? When in doubt, write it out. And, don't worry ... be happy.

CHAPTER 14

It's All in the Family

You're the heart of the human family, the
promise of life to come.
The pulse of the living world, you are the only
one.

—John St.Augustine

W ay back in 1993, I was teaching at Schurz High School in Chicago. I graduated from the same school, so it was a real kick to go back and *give back*—at least for a few years. One early September morning as I was signing in, I noticed a letter in my mailbox from the Windstar Foundation. Jackie and I had just returned from a symposium at Windstar in August, and this letter was announcing the theme for the 1994 event in Aspen, Colorado. A bold headline read: *Choices for the Future—The Human Family*. I tucked the letter in my bag and went off to class, but throughout the day I kept glancing at it: *The Human Family*. I would look at the many faces in the classroom in front of me—from so many different backgrounds and races—and the concept of this large, sprawling family began to work on my mind. Words began to form, and then a line here and a line there. Finally, by the time I arrived home, I had written a poem called "The Human Family." I had no idea that I would be standing on the stage of the Aspen Music Tent one year later reciting the words to that poem to a few thousand people from all over the world. It was truly a cross-section of the human family.

Maintaining the foundations of our families and preventing the degeneration of the family unit are some of the biggest challenges we face today. Few models remain of what working family dynamics look like here in the 21st century. It's possible we can find some answers from the last century, perhaps on Walton's Mountain.

Earl Henry Hamner, Jr., was born on July 10, 1923, to Earl Henry and Doris Hamner in Schuyler, Virginia. He was the oldest of eight red-haired children—three girls and five boys. Earl began his writing career at the age of 6, and his first poem, about puppies and a red wagon, was published on the children's page of *The Richmond Times Dispatch*. He graduated from Schuyler High School, went on to the University of Richmond on a scholarship, and was drafted into the army in 1943. Earl served in World War II until 1946. After the war, he got his start in show business at WMBG Radio in Richmond. I often kid Earl that he and Marconi, the "Father of Radio," must have had a great time together back in the day.

In 1946, Earl attended Northwestern University and was also a writer for WLW in Cincinnati from 1946 until 1948. In 1949, Earl headed to New York where he was a radio and television writer until 1960. Earl married Jane Martin, editor of *Harper's Bazaar*, on October 16, 1954, and they have been at each other's side for more than 50 years. In 1960, Earl moved to Hollywood to pursue film writing. His novel, *Spencer's Mountain*, was made into a movie starring Henry Fonda and Maureen O'Hara in 1963. *Spencer's Mountain* has also been published in ten languages.

In 1970, Earl was contacted by Lorimar Productions to write a television special based on his novella, *The Homecoming*. It was broadcast on CBS and starred Richard Thomas, Patricia Neal, and Edgar Bergen. The overwhelming response to the show was the inspiration for the series, *The Waltons*, starring Richard Thomas, Michael Learned, and Ralph Waite. The show aired from 1972 until 1981, touching the lives of millions of families around the world—and still does to this day. While *The Waltons* made Earl Hamner a household name, not many people know that he also wrote episodes for *The Twilight Zone* at the insistence of his old friend Rod Serling. Of all his achievements, Earl considers being chosen by E. B. White to do a film version of the children's classic *Charlotte's Web* right near the top of his high honors list.

Now nearing his 84th birthday, Earl Hamner not only gave the world a touching portrait of his family during The Great Depression, but he also provided a blueprint for families in general, no matter the challenges they face. Personally, one of the great delights of my life has been my friendship with the real-life John-Boy Walton, who has used my microphone to remind us of the old-fashioned values that never go out of fashion. But his lessons on the art of writing and his support of my literary efforts have been nothing short of incredible. Since this is my book—and my space—I want to take this opportunity to thank Earl for his role as one of America's great storytellers, and for encouraging me to forge ahead during the times when no one thought this book would find its way into a reader's hand.

I highly suggest you pick up a copy of *The Avocado Drive Zoo*. It's a funny, irreverent look at life through the eyes of Earl Hamner Jr. When the book was released in 1999, I jumped at the chance to have Earl on the show. Like so many others, I had sat around the living room with my folks to watch *The Waltons*, and I really connected with all the characters, and especially Earl's narration. There is something about his voice that hearkens back to warm summer days, sitting on a swing in the shade of a giant oak while sipping lemonade. That added to the anticipation of spending a bit of time with him.

On a recent show, Earl and I had a little conversation about the very big subject of family. It was just after the release of Jim Person, Jr.'s fine biography, *Earl Hamner: From Walton's Mountain to Tomorrow.*

I got the ball rolling by saying, "If there was room for one more face on Mt. Rushmore, perhaps we should consider carving in stone the features of Earl Hamner. Too bad we can't set up some kind of voice-response system so that when visitors come within a few hundred feet of your monument, they would hear, 'It was springtime on Walton's Mountain' in that Schuyler, Virginia, lilt. What do you think, Mr. Hamner?"

"If the purpose of Mt. Rushmore is tourism, I cannot imagine that I could draw any additional crowds. Now, if the purpose is in being a stoneface—that I can do on occasion!" Earl laughed.

"Earl, *The Waltons* aired for nine years and became a part of the fabric of America. Everyone was walking around saying, 'Good night, John-Boy,' even if their kid was named Sam. Did you have any idea that the book *Spencer's Mountain* would morph into one of the best-loved shows of all time? And what is it that you think attracts viewers then and now?"

"As a writer, I had already done some things that made it to television—*CBS Playhouse* and, of course, *The Twilight Zone*—but in Hollywood you never know what will happen or what will catch on. I will say that the timing of *The Waltons*, right at the end of the Vietnam War, was critical to its success. We wanted to get back to our roots, our families, and our heritage, much like America today. Perhaps that's why I still get a tremendous amount of mail, but not just from the United States. As a matter of fact, just this morning I received a letter from a young father in Calcutta. Can you believe that? He thanked me for the show and focusing on the family. It goes to show that mothers and fathers are the same in Indiana or India."

Earl continued, "I think that people still watch the show for a couple of reasons. First, it reminds them of simpler times. But just because it was simpler does not mean it was better or easier. All we had back then, as now, was each other. That is one of the things that never goes out of style—the need for humans to connect with one another. Second, I feel that *The Waltons* had such an impact on the culture because it was based on real events, not some made-up reality show that is on the television today. Each show was a lesson from my childhood, and people could apply it to their lives. I am not sure that a show I saw the other day, *Fear Factor*, is something that is going to help the family stay together. We have enough things to fear in the world today. I don't think we need a show about it." Earl said this as if we needed to be reminded of the silliness of some TV shows by a grandfather who knew the value of time well spent.

I asked Earl if he felt that the message of *The Waltons* had "stood up" to the electronic age that we now live in. How can it compete with video games, iPods, and cell phones?

"Well, the times are most definitely different than during the Depression, but the need for the family might be more important now than it was back then. Kids today have so many more dangers to be aware of and so many choices they need to make. Back on the mountain, we knew our neighbors—and their neighbors, too. Today, there seems to be just too much going on for young people to focus on enjoying life while they can. I don't know if the show can catch the attention of families anymore—not because they wouldn't like it, but because families are rarely together enough to sit down together. The world is just moving faster and faster every day. We make kids grow up so fast that the family finds itself out of balance."

I sensed more than a little sadness in Earl's tone, almost a wistfulness about yesteryear when, though things were difficult, it was a safer, more stable time for families.

Then Earl reversed his tone.

"Of course, you know that I wrote and produced the show *Falcon Crest*, which was sort of *The Waltons* gone bad, I suppose. It was about a ruthless family matriarch who would do just about anything to get her way. But in many ways, that show shed light on how different families can be. Even though they might seem to be dysfunctional, perhaps it was a good way to see how the family unit works under, let's say ... *different* circumstances. I don't get nearly the same amount of mail for that show as I do from *Waltons* fans."

While the times have changed, the need for family has not. Unfortunately, Earl is right on the mark in terms of the pace we keep and how hard it is on families in the 21st century. We have our kids signed up for every sport and activity available, but have a hard time communicating with them about the important things. When I was growing up in the '60s and '70s, my mom was home most every day when I hit the door after school. She worked part-time in the mornings so she could be there in the critical 3-to-6 P.M. time slot when so many kids go unsupervised and unnoticed. While we were a far cry from the Waltons, I did grow up with a sense of duty to family. Today, the things I like to do most involve just spending time at home with Jackie and the kids. Even though both of the kids are teenagers and would rather be out the door, we sit down to dinner at least three nights a week. It takes some doing, but it's an investment in communication.

One night last summer, I was doing my duty at the grill when the phone rang. I quickly checked caller ID. Earl Hamner, Jr.'s name was on the little screen.

"Just calling to check in, John. (Thankfully, he has never called me John-Boy *yet*.) How is the family doing? How are Amanda and Andrew?" Earl knew of my kids from the various online columns I have written over the years. I was frankly surprised that he remembered their names. Sometimes *I* forget them. We had a nice chat about what was going on in the world and, of course, the solutions to the ills of society, and it always seemed to bounce back to families—being part of them, recognizing and celebrating them, understanding them. Talking family matters with the gentle Virginian is like taking off your shoes and walking barefoot in the tall grass. It's about as natural as it gets.

Family, like the foundations of anything that is built to last, must be strong, yet flexible—and be filled with faith, strength, discipline and, most importantly, love for one another.

—Earl Hamner

Earl has a great sense of the human family, and has the evidence to back it up. More than 30 years after *The Waltons* found its way into the living rooms of America, a father in Calcutta writes him a letter of thanks for showing how a family could be. A man in Germany creates a *Waltons* home page. Earl's book signings are standing room only. My phone rings, and he is just checking in. It proves that whether we like to admit it or not, we are all connected. The theme of family—one of the most sacred connections we have—is not confined to a mountaintop in Virginia, but it is needed and revered around the world.

It's a Family Affair

When *The Waltons* aired in the '70s, it gained a huge following, but it also garnered critics who deemed the show "simplistic and not accurate in its portrayal of the times." I think they missed the point. It was a television show that had a strong theme of family running through it, and while sometimes life is not so simple, the concept of a family can and should be. We cannot turn back the hands of time, but we can bring yesterday's lessons into today. There might not be many "Walton-ish" families around with regard to size, but the structure is more important. Whether it's eight kids or one, whether Grandpa is still around or is acting as the father for whatever reason, families in this century have a whole new set of challenges in front of them that the kids in Schuyler, Virginia, could never have dreamed of. But the truth is, *kids are kids at the core*, and family is the one core concept we must support, define, and renovate lest we go the way of ancient Rome.

Earl Hamner is a true reflection of family because both are multifaceted. There is no cut-and-dried template on family. There is no one "best way" to define a family. Family is often a tug-of-war, a battle zone, and a peace accord—and that's just at dinner! In the same vein, Earl Henry Hamner, Jr. is more than just "Mr. Walton." I think what best exemplifies what the world needs now in regard to family comes from Earl himself in a speech he gave at the Walton's Mountain Museum in 1997. He spoke of the values that were the baseline themes of the show and times.

"They came from our parents, the people who nurtured us and passed on to us the notions that there was dignity in work, satisfaction in a job well done, that we can and must be self-reliant and resourceful, that our country's laws must be obeyed, that we have the right to practice the religion of our choice, the belief that our parents and grandparents not only deserve respect, but are to be treasured for the rituals and stories and rules of conduct that we all need to know and pass on to our children if we are to call ourselves civilized."

In short, family is the launching pad for the trip that all of us take to the stars. If there is no guidance system onboard, no sense of connection to those in our immediate family and the larger view of the human family, then the threads of disconnect and discontent begin to replace the strands of strength and sensibility. Then the one foundational unit that we base Western civilization on goes from "Good night, John-Boy" to *Trading Spouses* in the blink of an eye.

When all is said and done, family is the one source that teaches us the most lessons in life. You didn't choose the people in your family, but nonetheless you are stuck with them. Maybe applying a little "front-porch wisdom" is just the ticket. And by the way, next time you have a little time on your hands, find out if *The Waltons* is airing on a station near you. I guarantee it will be time well invested and a great little reminder of what so many long for—family.

Time Is Really, Really Important

I could have sworn when I woke up this morning that I was still a bright-eyed young man with nary a care in the world, but the reality is that I am a 47-year-old husband and father of two with the weight of the universe on my shoulders every day. Steve Miller captured this phenomenon in *Fly Like an Eagle:* "Time keeps on slippin' slippin' slippin' into the future...." Time is the one thing that families seem to never have enough of, but need more of. It might take a concentrated effort on your part to carve out time, but it might be easier than you think. Turn off the television for a couple of hours. Don't answer the phone. Pull out a board game. Read the comics together. You can never regain the time you have lost—period—but you can make the most of the time you have left together.

Give Each Other Space

The Waltons didn't all get along, and neither do we. But what's important is to allow space for family members to be who they are, no matter how troubling it sometimes gets. (I am not talking about criminal behavior here.) Lessons and family are tightly intertwined, and while sometimes we think one of our brothers or sisters is off track, it's quite possible they are on the right track to learn something they would have missed if their path had been different. We tend to see things through our own eyes and experiences only, and while we may be correct in our assessment of a situation, it's quite possible that things need to be the way they are *for people to become who they can.* This is sometimes tough to accept, but essential if we are to allow others to discover who they are and how they fit into the family . . . and the world.

More Than One Family

With a divorce rate hovering around 50 percent, the definition of family has radically changed over the years, and will continue to do so. But just because families have changed, it does not mean that the importance of connection and grounding and love has to. If you are in a situation where there is more than one father or mother in a family (and you may be one of them), make sure your focus stays on being happy, instead of just being right. The world is filled with misery, so don't add to it. If you absolutely must pound each other over the head, don't do it in your home. Go rent some "sumo suits" (these are huge foam bodies you put on complete with Sumo attire) and have fun ramming yourselves into oblivion. Don't settle arguments with verbal abuse or threats of the lowest level. Find common ground and show your kids how to be responsible adults. Don't just do what you know; do what you can.

Adopt-a-Family

There are signs all around the country for adopt-a-highway groups whose job is to go out on occasion and clean up the debris the rest of us toss away. One great way to get a better perspective on family is to spend time with kids who don't really have one. Through the Big Brothers/Big Sisters organization, I meet once a week with a little guy named Tyler at his school for just 30 minutes. I am just as busy as the next person, but I have found that I need that half-hour break away from the adult world, and it does my soul good to see the world through the eyes of a sixth-grader at least once a week. You don't have to go through the full adoption process, but I highly suggest you contact your local BB/BS group and sign up for corporate mentoring. Most of these kids just need a little boost. Their home situations may be tough or nonexistent, and your presence can make a world of difference. Unfortunately, garbage is not the only thing that is tossed aside. Kids are, too, and you can do something about it. Thirty minutes can change a life—maybe even yours.

It's Really All of Us

I started out this chapter with the concept of the human family—6 billion strong and growing larger every year. For the most part, we do all right, but now and then one of us gets *middle-child syndrome* or *baby-of-the-family syndrome* or *nobody-ever-pays-attention-to-me syndrome,* and the next thing you know, the world is paying attention again—usually through a lot of pain and misery. For every Mahatma Gandhi who "gets it," there is a Hitler who tries to "undo it." It is a constant push and pull for the human family, and until we find our place in it, we fail to see that, like it or not, we are all connected. In order to be an effective member of the human family, we must first make sure we have ourselves in order. *When we are responsible for ourselves, we are better able to help others.* There are too many of us running around doing the opposite—trying to be responsible for everybody else and not for ourselves first. You can't give what you don't have. The ripple effect is based on the fact that everything emanates from a nucleus and spreads outward. If that nucleus does not have all its parts functioning, then the ripple that spreads will reflect the energy put forth in a negative way, and if it's from a good, positive, loving core, the result will be one of a much higher nature. But both affect the whole of things—the family all of us are a part of. I have been very fortunate in my life to have a large family, perhaps not biologically, but rather spiritually. I consider the people in this book to be part of that family. In fact, my friends are sometimes closer than blood relations. The first step in taking your place in the human family is acknowledging that there is one. . . . *Welcome home.*

Human Family

Have you ever sat in wonder at the setting of the sun?
Or how a flower blossoms and that summer always comes?
Ever held a snowflake or dried a small child's tears?
Ever dreamed of peace and love throughout your living years?
You're the heart of the Human Family, the promise of life to come
The pulse of the living world, you are the only one.
Have you ever walked in the rain?
Smelling the sweetness of drops in the wind?
Ever knelt in humble prayer in forgiveness of imagined sin?
Ever hurt so bad that you swear you'd really rather die?
And woke the next morning to see rainbows in the sky?
You're the eyes of the Human Family, the promise of life to come
A prophet of faith and giver of dreams, you are the only one.
Have you ever seen the hunger in the children of the land?
And watched as we consume ourselves—destroying what we don't
    understand?
Ever stood in silence as the leaders slowly take their fall?
Praying for their legacy and all the names on cold stone walls.
You're the voice of the Human Family, the promise of life to come
Singer of songs for all the world, and your greatest has yet to be sung.
On this day sit in wonder at the miracle you truly are
Know that your light shines from the heaven within
And is as bright as the midnight star.
Dream of a world without hunger where the children never shed
    cruel tears.
Know that you can make that happen by living through untrue fears.
We are the Human Family, with footsteps in the sand.
We are the Human Family, walking hand in hand.
We are the Human Family, responsible for all we see.
We are the Human Family; the truth will set us free.

—**John St. Augustine**

CHAPTER 15

Coming Out of the Dark

*I am not bound to win, but I am bound to be
true. I am not bound to succeed, but I am
bound to live up to what light I have.*

—Abraham Lincoln

As I write this, it's springtime here in Upper Michigan, at least according to the date, not the weather. Winter seems to be taking its time in leaving, as if it wants to be remembered as long as possible. But in the next few weeks, the buds on the trees will awaken, and the grasses and flowers will come out of their dormancy, once again ushering in a new season. On the heels of the colored flora bursting forth will be a long line of birds, critters, and flying things waiting for their turn at nature's feast.

In the side yard, I have a small flowerbed. I'm hoping I planted the tulip bulbs deep enough to withstand the snow and cold. Each day when I leave home, I glance toward that little patch of earth that is marked by four railroad ties and a glass sun face on a metal pole. The snow is slow to leave that part of the yard because it's closer to the hill, so it takes that much longer for the sun to do its thing. I resist the urge to get out a shovel and clear the snow from the garden, thinking that if I did so the tulips would show up just a little faster and would coax spring to arrive before its time.

Often our lives are just like that garden—sometimes full of color and abundance; other times, gray, dormant, and waiting. Deep inside each of us is a seed that might take years to burst forth—but when it does, the whole world takes notice.

Maureen Moss is a cultivator of seeds. She never intended to be a writer, motivational speaker, or personal coach, but after 20 successful years in the business world, she was far from feeling fulfilled and knew something had to change. Maureen began expanding her horizons to include speaking about what she knew as a businesswoman and a resourceful human being. Still, something was missing. Maureen told her friends that she felt as though a panther dwelled inside, scratching at her soul, trying to get out. Like so many others who have felt that deep gnawing within, she went in search of the key to living a life of purpose.

Maureen began to investigate what was inside—besides the panther pacing back and forth. For more than a dozen years, she engaged in the greatest adventure—internal excavation. She became certified in various courses of study regarding the world of inner significance and began to transform into a more substantial human being. Her willingness to let the part of her that was seeking refuge in "the great external promise" slowly die off was a rebirth on many levels.

Leaving the business world a piece at a time, Maureen turned her focus to people who were struggling to find their peace. As a personal coach and teacher, she began working with a wide variety of people from many walks of life—judges, nurses, teachers, CEOs, married couples, single mothers, families in crisis, and homeless children. Proving that what you do is not as important as who you are, for the first time in her life she was living up to her true inner self.

Besides public speaking, Maureen began writing her first book. *The Nature of Bliss: Balance, Love, Integrity, Sexuality, Soul* was the result of her years of walking the inner path and discovering that the dormant parts of her self had begun to awaken. The seeds of change were working their way to the surface.

I am not sure who sent me the book—and it really doesn't matter—but it was the leap-off point for not only some incredible radio shows, but perhaps more importantly for a friendship that seems on so many levels to have ancient roots.

After doing thousands of radio shows, I am pretty accurate at reading guests—what motivates them, understanding their speech patterns, knowing what it will take to prod them into not only delivering their message, but also a great performance that will keep listeners' attention. Just because someone is a great writer does not mean they are wonderful conversationalists. During Maureen's first appearance on my show, any concerns I might have had about her energy, ability to communicate, or motivation went right out the studio door. I am convinced that Maureen has a fuse somewhere that she lights right after she wakes up in the morning, and it sets off energy bombs about every two minutes. The woman is walking spiritual dynamite!

I took to simply calling her "M," not only to sound like I was in a James Bond movie, but also because it just seemed to fit someone whose first and last name begin with the same letter. Mine do not, but nonetheless I became "J" to her, and we were off to the races.

Because Maureen's energy and message are more than one radio segment long, we took to pulling apart her book once a month over a year-long period. At one point, we landed on the subject of transformation and what each of us can become if we allow ourselves to participate in the process.

Maureen had this to say: "Humanity is in the process of shedding thousands of years of spiritual rust from our souls. We have been told since nearly the beginning of time that we are not good enough or strong enough or smart enough or talented enough or pretty enough. I say enough is enough!

"The word 'transformation' means a change in composition or structure. We have been led to believe that this can be accomplished from the outside in—and it can be if you want the results to last until the first payment book arrives in the mail or you see a better pair of shoes in the window. So we mostly go through our lives on the mouse wheel—running without even knowing why, chasing some elusive idea of what we think life should be. And we wouldn't even know if we arrived there because we have not taken the time to figure out who we are in relation to what we seek. But there is another option—call it Plan B if you want—because I am here to tell you that Plan A isn't working very well.

"Consider the butterfly. We see this beautiful creature only at the final stage of its growth, after it has gone through a transformation or change in structure that starts on the inside. It goes through four stages of change before it is capable of flying. It all starts with an egg, of course, and then comes the larva or caterpillar chewing its way through leaves and grass. Its only job at this point is to feed itself in preparation for the next stage. Caterpillars grow almost 100 times in size during this feeding frenzy, and they actually store food for later use as an adult. When it has eaten enough, it goes into the third stage, which is the resting or transformational period. A cocoon is formed. From all outward appearances, nothing is going on, but on the inside—where it really counts—big things are happening. This stage of development can last from a few weeks to a few months and even a few years. Finally, and right on time, the adult butterfly emerges, dries its wings, and flies off to become part of the cycle again."

I listened to this biology lesson—one familiar to all of us—but somehow it sounded like the first time I had ever heard it. The applications to our lives seemed more than obvious.

"M, is there one stage that is more important than the others?" I asked.

"Well, J, it would seem they are all essential to producing the result, but perhaps the one that humans fear the most is the cocoon stage, where we have to go inside ourselves to become something different. It means removing yourself from the world you are familiar with and being with just yourself. Most people hate that part."

"Why?"

"Because we don't know who we are, and we have tied our identity up to all the outer things in life. Dropping all that seems like a death of sorts. What people don't know—and butterflies do—is that the only way you can go from crawling to flying is by internal transformation. We are afraid to go in because we fear we might never come out again. And to some degree, that is true. The person who goes through an internal structural change is not the same human who went in—and that is exactly the point."

"So, it's like we are afraid of the dark?" I asked.

"No, we are afraid of the light," she answered.

Bingo. As previously noted in these pages, one of the most excruciating decisions I have ever made was to "pull the plug" on my show in December 2002. As the day drew nearer, my anxiety increased a hundredfold. How in the world could I stop doing what seemed to be "ordained" in so many ways? I had investors who thought enough of my work to back it, and I felt a deep responsibility to them, even though there were no guarantees the show would be picked up nationally and their investment would pay off. I had a family to support, medical bills to pay and, perhaps more than anything else, it felt to me that if I were to stop, there would be no other chance for me to regain what I had worked so hard for.

After doing an afternoon of shows, I closed the office door and simply lay on the carpet and broke down. I looked at the countless books that all promised a better life. I thought about the many authors and leaders with whom I had conversed. I reflected on the people who listened in daily and felt like I had failed—again.

Then the phone rang. It was Maureen Moss—just a coincidence, I'm sure.

It didn't take long for her to figure out what sort of state I was in. We spoke for a long time about the power of surrender and how important faith is when it comes to our dreams and desires. Then she took me back to Butterfly Biology 101.

"J, there is no doubt in my mind that you are entering a cocoon stage. I understand your fear, which mostly has to do with being responsible to people other than yourself. But I am here to tell you that if you don't go through this transition, you will not be any good to anyone. I know that you are going to come out the other end of this tunnel ready to fly higher than ever before, and you will look back at this time as truly essential to your unfolding future."

I remained in the cocoon for 33 months, coming out now and then to test my wings. I grew inside and found places I did not know even existed. I spent a lot of time alone and began to learn to trust the process—to not push the river, but to let the inner work move in me as it needed to. An immeasurable amount of strength is gained in that cocoon stage—a strength that is needed to break free of the constraints of yesterday and embrace the promise of today.

Maureen and I spoke frequently during my self-imposed hiatus. She was always encouraging, reminding me and reinforcing that the process always works in its perfect time. In one conversation, she excitedly shared with me her newly discovered concept she termed Troubled Mind Syndrome (TMS).

"Given the amount of information that we are asked to consider on a daily basis, there is no doubt in my mind—which is not troubled at the moment—that we are slowly being consumed by our technological age. There is no escape from the negative and non-informing news that is shoved down our mental drain pipe, resulting in greater levels of depression, suicide, and pessimism," Maureen said.

"What's the treatment? Is there a cure? Since you have discovered the problem, there must be a solution built into it," I suggested.

"The cure is to do what it says in the Bible: don't be conformed to the world, but be transformed by the renewing of your mind," M said. "The answer has been around for thousands of years, but it's no match for technology. The bottom line is that either we are going to conform the technology to fit our needs and desires, or technology is going to conform us to fit its application in our lives."

Amen to that. A myriad of choices confront us every day. Diet or regular? Left or right? Decaf or full strength? What's for dinner? The confused mind wants to provide solutions, but like a giant drain pipe, it's clogged big time. We have become conditioned to make choices that are not essential to our survival, like the ones mentioned above and a jillion others that are just filler materials. We spent $20 billion on headache remedies last year, and I predict that number will increase as we create more and more diversions from who we really are.

When I returned to the air in 2005, Maureen and I picked up right where we left off and talked about her latest work, *Commitment to Love: Transforming Human Nature into Divine Nature*. She took listeners back to the basics of the evolution of the butterfly, but with an added message: "Trusting the process also means trusting the source that created the process. In the final stage, the butterfly takes flight because it has a new power source, if you will; one that was not fully developed while it was just a crawling larva. As it grew in size, so did it grow in knowing that its destiny was to become more than it had ever been. Transforming human nature into divine nature asks us to do the same—to move away from the human things who drive us and re-connect with the divine energy that lifts us above the chaos and closer to the flowers that life has to offer. And you know what, J? There isn't anyone on the planet who isn't capable of becoming more than they are. You just have to be willing to let go of who you *think* you are, which is directed by the troubled mind, and act on the guidance that tells the caterpillar inside all of us to just hang in there. Before long, you will find your wings."

Transition is an earned privilege that each of us has a right to.
You will either move up or stay put, depending on your commitment to transcending the limits of lower thought and ego
by developing a higher consciousness and accepting the divinity that is your birthright.

—Maureen Moss

Earning Your Wings

At one time, I thought I knew everything because there was no reason to question the world in which I lived. "Right" and "wrong" were easy choices. Nothing challenged my definitions, so maintaining them took little effort. Then life began to intervene, sometimes in very subtle ways. Take relationships, for example. How I viewed them and how my partner viewed them were quite different at times. The definition I had grown up with, which made up my blueprint, was sometimes in stark contrast to the relationship that I was actually engaged in. It was no longer an issue of how it *should* be, but a new experience of how it *could* be—if I was open to the concept of transformation or inner structural change.

Every area of our lives is undergoing transformation, but we are seldom conscious enough to recognize it. Our cells restructure themselves over and over again, repairing and restoring every second we are alive. Technology is transforming our habits. Ten years ago, a Web site was something a spider created. Now, if you don't have one, your "online presence" suffers. You could never have convinced my dad that the schlocky gadgets he got such a kick out of in *Star Trek* would someday be a part of our lives. My flip cell phone looks strangely similar to Captain Kirk's communicator. Ideas and concepts are the building blocks of transformation, so then it stands to reason that if you carefully consider the ideas that have shaped your life and the concepts that you have employed to carry out those ideas, you arrive at the roots of transformation. If you then let that lead you through the cocoon phase of your life, the end result will be assured upon your emergence.

Built into every lowly, crawling larva is a butterfly. Just because you can't see the wings doesn't mean they aren't there. Here are a few reminders as you progress from earthbound worm to heaven-sent monarch. (Thanks, M.)

This Isn't It

Can you imagine trying to tell a larva that someday it will break the bonds of earth and flutter effortlessly on the wind? It's like trying to tell a human who has made the same mistake over and over again that it's just part of the journey. Where you are at this moment *isn't the final verdict for your life.* Unless your remains have already been taken care of, there are still paths to explore, leaves to chew, and flowers in need of pollination. Maureen Moss went from being a very successful businesswoman to a very successful author, but she had to endure the same steps that nature has laid out for the butterfly. Unless you choose to be a worm your whole life, you have to follow the grand design. Take a moment to see where you are on the path: Seed? Larva? Stuck on the front of a semi-truck? Sometimes you are the windshield, and sometimes you are the bug—or the butterfly in this case.

It's All about Cycles

Not the kind you ride, but the kind you live. The average American will go through seven career changes in a lifetime. The days of working 40 years at the same plant are pretty much gone. Transformation means change, and if there is one certainty it's that we will live a life of change—and a lot of "small lives." We are always going through a cycle of some kind—beginnings, middles, and endings with jobs, children, spouses, homes, you name it. Recognizing that the life cycle is not something you live outside of—but rather inside of—takes the edge off things. The fear factor is lessened. It's been said you can be either a victim of change or a participant, but not both, and certainly not at the same time. What cycle are you in today? (Re-cycling does not count, but on behalf of landfills everywhere, thank you.)

Give It Up

Here's the deal: Resisting the inevitable is an exercise in futility. The process of transformation excludes no one. The only question is: How hard will you fight the changes that are manifesting in your life? What will it take to embrace them? We are a world filled with people who desperately wish their lives were different in some way. And yet when the universe presents options (that may look at the time like closed doors, lost love, and empty bank accounts), we balk at the idea of having to change within. Every outer circumstance is manifest from an inner place, and if that place does not include transformation, then you remain a leaf-munching green worm that is food for birds. To tell the truth, even when you transform, you are food for birds—you just look better. Be open to the transformation that is being placed in your path. It makes the time in the cocoon that much easier.

It's "Chrysalis" Clear

I'm getting tired of using the word "cocoon," so on to the big words. At this stage in a butterfly's development, the full-grown caterpillar has holed up in a shell of sorts called a *chrysalis*. You have seen them hanging from trees, under roofs, or in a jar in third-grade science. The technical term for the caterpillar at this point is a *pupa* as it is within the protection of the cocoon. Pupa is very close to the word *pupil*, and that is what going into the *cocoon stage* of the life cycle is all about—learning from within.

Before M started writing books and speaking to groups all over the world, she went within—and stayed there until the lessons were clear. As for me, after crawling as a caterpillar (I thought I was flying, but I wasn't even close), it took a 33-month sentence in the chrysalis for me to grow a new, stronger set of wings that could hold my newly found perspective on what was possible. It's going to get dark in there.

It's going to be scary. It's going to be suffocating and confining and dull and lonely. There is only room for one in a cocoon. Your world is going to seem like it's been turned upside down—and it has, for a very good reason. Your best friend during this time is a pad of paper and a pencil. Record your thoughts, fears, and feelings, so later you cannot only get a good laugh, but also see how far you have come.

Take Off

So you spend some time inside going through the dark night of the soul, and you are getting itchy because you can feel something going on inside. One day, the fear just leaves—and in its place is the kind of faith needed to gain altitude against all odds. It is the kind of faith that hovers over life's challenges, that says, "I always knew you had it *in* you." The re-emergence is a critical stage of transformation. Breaking free from the chrysalis requires a little patience on your part. When it's time to come out, you'll know it. Coming out of the dark and into the light requires an awareness of the journey—the stages and the results. Most importantly, make sure you remind the next caterpillar you run across that his or her future includes a flight plan—and be willing to share yours.

There are no hard-and-fast rules for the transformation process except one: no one is exempt from the opportunity unless they choose to not participate in life. If you are here, eventually you get the chance to stop crawling and start flying. And then a whole new world, from an entirely different perspective, awaits.

CHAPTER 16

One Step at a Time

Success is always temporary. When all is said and done, the only thing you'll have left is your character.

—Vince Gill

When I was a kid, one of the most popular shows on TV was *Let's Make a Deal*. Contestants would dress up in goofy outfits and, if chosen, they had the chance to pick from several offerings and make the best deal they could. To me, the best part of the show was when host Monty Hall would say, "You can keep the toaster or choose the box where the lovely Carol Merrill is standing." We would shout at the television, exhorting some guy dressed as a mailbox with dollar bills stuffed in it to forgo the endless pockets on Monty's jacket and see what was behind the big green box on the stage.

Life is just like *Let's Make a Deal*. All of us are trying to stand out from the crowd and find out what kind of deal life has in store for us. But unlike many of the contestants on the show, most of us do not choose to give up the security in hand for the chance of a lifetime behind curtain number three. It takes real character to move forward despite all outward appearances and find your place in the world.

- 173 -

One of the great things about doing a show like mine is the transference of energy that takes place when I am spending time with a guest. I could be going into the studio after spending the day on a million other things not connected to radio, but as soon as I flip that switch, a new gear kicks in. Add stimulating conversation that actually leads to higher levels of awareness and, *man*, you know it's what you were born to do. I hold the vibration between the microphone and the listener as a sacred space, leaving the schlocky stuff to the lower life forms on the dial and proceeding with what I know we need now more than ever—material that builds character.

The 21 people in this book each represent a specific lesson about living an uncommon life. Character would have to be right near the top of the list of those lessons. These people have come to know that character is built step by step and through those famous "character-building days" we all enjoy so much. A few of the definitions of *character* include a distinctive quality or attribute of a person, one's stance or firmness of being. My favorite description comes from the Greek root *charassein*, and it means "to engrave." When you come across people who have character engraved on their soul, you know it. There is a certainty and solidness to their presence, and you can feel that each step along their journey has left its mark. One man who has made his mark in my life and those of many others is Hal Thau.

Hal and Dorothy Thau now split their time between Aspen and New York City, but Hal grew up in what he calls "the upholstered sewers (small nightclubs, joints) of New York." A rough-and-tumble early life gave him an appreciation for hard work, steadfast friendships, and looking at life as a journey to be explored to the fullest. Hal knows all about pulling back the curtains of opportunity. An accomplished theater producer, businessman, consultant, and author, Hal defines what character is all about. Growing up in the East Bronx, Hal dreamed of making his way in the world. Little did he know back then that his dreams would take him from the back alleys of Brooklyn to the Great Wall of China and beyond.

One trait of character is the ability to take that which may seem chaotic and put it in some semblance of order. This sounds easier than it is. With years of filling the role of accountant and business manager to the stars, finding ways to straighten things out was a moment-by-moment challenge for Hal. It was the death of his father Morris at the young age of 45 that prepared Hal for the work that lay ahead. Morris Thau was a free spirit, and like many young men of his time, he was looking for his own pot of gold. Shortly after WWII started, Morris began accepting orders to ship foodstuff overseas from his already established deli, and the business really took off. Morris took in a partner, but the guy was a crook and was skimming off the accounts. Soon, there was no money left, and things went downhill quickly. Morris lost his footing on the ladder of prosperity and could not regain his place. No one in the family knew that, in order to keep things afloat, Morris had borrowed money from a loan shark. A knock at the door after Morris passed away taught a young Harold Thau to quickly learn how to make order out of chaos—a trait that would serve him throughout his life.

That one lesson would translate into a journey that put Hal in the lives of some of America's greatest entertainers, movers and shakers. John Malkovich, Burl Ives, Judith Light, Peter, Paul and Mary, Nina Simone, Billy Strayhorn, Joni Mitchell, Tom Paxton, Jackie Vernon, "Cannonball" Adderley, and Jerry Stiller and Anne Meara are just a few of the people who have been in Hal's life as friends, clients, and confidants. Being a business manager to high-profile people is not as glamorous as it sounds. Very creative people can also be self-destructing people at times, and Hal's down-to-earth, grounded New York style has saved more than one celebrity's backside.

As previously mentioned, I was asked by John Denver to speak at his Windstar Foundation "Choices for the Future" Symposium in 1994. After my talk, I was astonished to see a line of over 100 people waiting behind the Aspen music tent to talk to me. I was stunned, to say the least. As I headed out to the meeting area, I bumped into Hal and his family backstage. There was a brief introduction that I am sure Hal doesn't even remember, but sometimes the universe puts puzzle pieces in place for a later connection.

Three years later, John Denver was gone, and one of my concerns was that people would forget his incredible talent and impact on the world, and not just with his music. I decided to do a tribute show on the one-year anniversary of Denver's passing, and the response was incredible as people phoned in from all over the world to share their thoughts about the man and his music.

When the thought came for a second anniversary show, I had the overwhelming urge to contact Hal, whom I knew really only in name and from a handshake in a hallway. I contacted his son Michael at Plant-It-2020, got Hal's number, and left him a message. A few days later, he called. We talked, and he agreed to share his perspective of a 30-year friendship with JD on the air. Once again, we did not have time for the callers who phoned in from all over America wanting to talk about Denver's impact on their lives. When the show finished, Hal told me that he was going to Chicago for theater business in the near future, and it turned out that I was going back there at the same time. We agreed to meet again shortly before the 1999 holiday season.

I figured Hal was tied up as we failed to connect on the last day before I was heading back home to Michigan. I was 50 miles away from Chicago when Hal found me at the home of my good friends, Ron and Jackie Eberle. I am not sure exactly how he found me, but I drove back to the city and met Hal and Dorothy for dinner. It was a wonderful evening, and we talked about family, radio, and the man who put the two of us together again—Mr. Denver.

As I drove them to their hotel, Hal offered to have my family spend some time with him and Dorothy in Aspen. I politely thanked them, but honestly felt it was nothing more than a nice gesture. Subsequent phone conversations proved his invitation to be sincere, and we made plans to head out in the summer of 2000.

We loaded up the van and headed out west, making our way into the mountains and up through Independence Pass. My kids still talk about the climb up that narrow, two-lane road. We arrived on a Sunday evening, and the welcoming spirit in Hal's home was akin to standing in a summer shower: it felt just right. We spent the better part of the week running around Aspen, and the kids ate up the clean mountain air. In particular, my son Andy took a shine to Hal's dog Ollie, and the two of them were inseparable for the entire week.

On the final night before we were supposed to leave, Hal and I retired to his office. With a great Merlot between us, we had one of the most important conversations I have ever engaged in. Hal sat back in his chair, sized me up, and said, "What's on your mind, big guy?"

I responded point-blank. "What the hell am I doing here? This is great and everything, but I am not sure how or why all this has come together."

Hal said, "Look, you have important work to do in the world. You have talent for connecting with people at their core. That is a very rare thing. I told Dorothy the first time I talked to you that I had a feeling about you. Big things are coming your way."

I did not know what to say. This is a guy who has worked with everyone from Duke Ellington to John Malkovich, and he was telling me that I was going in the right direction? I took another sip of Merlot and thought maybe I should listen. We talked far into the night about goals and dreams, aspirations and business. It seemed I learned more in those few hours about character than I had my entire life up to that point. You could tell by Hal's words that he knew who he was and, maybe more importantly, where he was from. When I mentioned that Aspen is a long way from the Bronx, he smiled and said, "Not as far as you think, and the trip has been worth it."

Character is like the stabilizer bar on your car. It's there to keep you going straight and true when the road gets bumpy and full of potholes. The only school I know of that offers a course on character is called life. We all go through a myriad of experiences that are like the proverbial grindstone used to sharpen a knife. The stone rotates the same for all, but it's how you position yourself that either sharpens you up or takes the edge right off.

Character is an earned thing. For some, it is built in a single moment, like standing at the front door of your home in a tough neighborhood as a young man, face to face with a thug who wants his money. For others, character is honed over a lifetime through the trials and tribulations that life offers as an opportunity to become a better human being than we were the day before.

I recall one event that really put Hal's character or "engraving" in perspective for me. Most of the guests I talk to do the show as a "phoner"—they call in from their homes or offices, or from the road while doing a book signing. (Twice, Wayne Dyer did the show on his cell while jogging on the beach in Florida, but it's not the recommended mode of conversation.) So when someone is actually able to be in the studio with me, it's a real treat.

Josh White, Jr., whose father was the famed blues artist and songwriter of "House of the Rising Sun," was in upper Michigan performing on various stages, and we extended an invitation to spend an hour with him on the air to talk about his music, his father's legacy, and anything else we could come up with. Josh is an American original. His music speaks to the heart of people, and when the great vocal coach in the sky was handing out pipes, he gave Josh an incredible set. In an age of teenagers voting for their favorite idol, Josh White, Jr. is a guardian for the roots of our collective musical heritage. Ironically, his work has had the "fountain of youth" effect on him: the man is 66 as of this writing, but looks and acts like a man in his 40s. Maybe we all should pick up a guitar at some point.

So Josh was in the studio and, unbeknownst to him, I had just finished talking with Hal about his upcoming event at the Denver Center called *Almost Heaven: Songs and Stories of John Denver*. This was a musical based on Denver's work that Hal produced and would eventually go on for a long, successful run in Colorado and then off-Broadway. Sitting in the studio was a copy of Hal's book, *Bronx to Broadway: A Life in Show Business*. As I was getting Josh settled in, I happened to notice the back cover of Hal's book, which is a montage of names with whom Hal has worked in entertainment. Immediately, something caught my eye... Anne Meara... Jerry Stiller... *Josh White Jr*. ... Hold on a second. I looked at Josh, then back to the book, and then back to Josh.

"Hey, do you know a gentleman named Hal Thau?"

A huge grin opened on Josh's face, jutting his formidable beard toward me.

"Hal! I haven't seen Hal in years! How do you know him?"

"He just finished the first hour with me from Aspen."

"You've got to be kidding me! When I was working the circuit in the '60s and '70s, Hal handled some of my business affairs. The thing I remember most about Hal was his professionalism, dedication and, most of all, *character*. He is a rare guy."

Character.

I called Hal right back and put him on the phone with Josh (what are the odds of this all happening?), and they spent a few minutes getting reacquainted. We actually did a segment with both of them on the air. It was a great show.

In the time since then, Hal has been one of my "go-to" people— and there are just a few of those. These are people who understand what I am going for on *and* off the air. They are people who don't just want to talk to me because I can help them sell books or move a product or give them a platform for their opinions. They are people of character—

those who deep down "get it" because they have "lived it." They are people who will go the extra mile, taking it step by step, from starting out with nothing in a small office in New York to arranging the behind-the-scenes details for a folk group in the '60s, to standing firmly behind one of the world's most beloved and familiar voices in the '70s, as well as a slew of other notable entertainers and achievers.

While life might be like a box of chocolates—*you never know what you are going to get,* as Forrest Gump would say—character is always on the mark, unwavering and straightforward, forged out of lonely nights at the desk, longer days on the road, and even on the deck of a mountain home in Aspen. It might be a long way from the Jennings Street Markets in the Bronx for Hal Thau, but every step was worth it as it has been for so many others who have been touched by his life.

As I look back on my life, I can see points on the map that looked like an opportunity disguised as hard work and dedication to a purpose. Anyone can do what I have done. You might not always know where you are going, but sometimes it's more important not to forget where you came from.

—Hal Thau

Stay in Character

It would be too easy to point out the seeming lack of character in society today, and while it's tempting, it would not be totally accurate. While the tabloids and televisions of America are filled with features and shows that do very little to encourage good character, there are in fact multitudes of people who do exhibit good character. Twenty-one of them are in this book. It does seem at times like we are more interested in *being a character* than in *having character*, but there is one major difference between these two concepts: *acting like a character comes and goes*, but *having character never leaves you, especially when you need it most—in the tough calls of life.*

Often we look for something in others that we think we do not have in ourselves, as if somehow they got a few genes that we did not. Nothing could be further from the truth. One of the greatest lessons I have learned in this gig called life is that we can only recognize in others what we have within us as well. Otherwise, we would have no reference point from which to work.

So, take heart. You don't have to take a course or download a video or buy a subscription to attain character. It comes as standard equipment at birth. It's been "engraved" in you as part of your spiritual DNA, but has most likely "rusted over" by the many challenges you have faced on the journey. Rust accumulates when something sits for long periods of time without movement, without use. Every time you play small, every time you sell out, or every time you seek the shortcut, rust builds up. But when you step up, speak up, and get up, character becomes your calling card.

If all the world's a stage, then more than likely you are the agent, ticket taker, prop person, usher, star of the show, and, of course, janitor. No matter what role you play or what position you have, character is the best supporting cast you could ever have.

Take It as It Comes

Life is not fair. If you have not figured that out by now, not much else in this book can be of any assistance. There are going to be times that test every fiber of your being. People of character are fully aware that they may not be able to control the events of their lives, but they are in charge of their response to those events. Life is set up as a growing process. Every new season brings growth, and humans are not outside the cycle of change (even though we would like to think so). Instead of whining when something comes your way that doesn't fit your idea of how things should be (of course, a little pressure release is allowed), face it head-on, stare it down, and see it for what it is. Character is built on the hard times of life, not the easy ones, so ducking punches actually can make you weaker, not stronger.

Seek It Out

If you are developing any part of your life, mentoring is a great way to grow. The people in this book are always here between the covers for you to refer to. In addition, find someone who exudes character and is accessible to you. Winning is contagious, but so is losing, so choose wisely the person from whom you will study and learn. Be straightforward when you approach the person with whom you would like to spend time. Tell him you admire the way he lives his life and ask if you can have a conversation about how and why he does what he does. Then listen, take notes, or record it so that when you feel like taking the easy way out, you will have evidence on hand for doing what needs to be done.

Shoulder the Load

The most effective way to get stronger is to do the work. Are you accustomed to shirking duties or situations that call for you to be in a position to show the rest of us what real character looks, feels, and acts like? Many people are not willing to step up because they are not sure of their ability to get the job done. Look at it this way: if the bozos who ran Enron into the ground can make it to the top of the corporate ladder before spending a million on doggie toys, you are more than able to organize a block party, run for school council president, start a business from scratch, or be a role model of character for your kids. The more repetitions you do, the stronger you get (and better looking!).

Don't Back Down

Remember the words to this Tom Petty song: *"Well, I know what's right. I got just one life in a world that keeps on pushing me around, but I'll stand my ground . . . and I won't back down."* That's character. More than a few people have forgotten what character is, and they act accordingly. They will do anything to bring people of character down so they'll feel better about themselves. When you know who you are and where you came from, there is no getting pushed around. I am not talking about armed conflict, but rather human conduct. Don't play games with people, and don't get involved with people who do. Majoring in minor things keeps you small. Majoring in major things technically makes you not only a ... *major* ... but also a person of high moral character. And that beats mind games every single time.

Build Up Your Clout

Josh White, Jr. had not seen Hal Thau in more than 20 years, but he remembered him for his *character*, among other things. Being a person of character is contagious. It's what people take away from you and carry with them. Like Vince Gill's quote at the beginning of this chapter, after all is said and done—and it will be—all that is left is the impression or "engraving" you leave with other people. While it's true that you have only one chance to make a first impression, it's also true that you will spend a lifetime in relationships with all kinds of people, and the one thing that will keep them coming back above all is character. Think about it: every single connection you have with someone, personally or professionally, is built on character. You cannot sustain successful relationships without it, and since the world is really nothing but one big block party, get about the business of character building. We could really use your help out here. Our reputation may always precede us, but our character defines us.

Take a minute to write down the name of one person—living or dead—who defines what you think character is all about. Then go look in the mirror. What do you see?

CHAPTER 17

No Faith in Fear

I figured out there's not too many limitations—if you do life your way.

—Johnny Cash

In his wisdom-filled song "Spanish Pipe Dream," singer/songwriter John Prine exhorts us to *"blow up your TV, throw away the paper, move to the country and build you a home."* Not much I can say with regard to the moving and homebuilding, but I am on board when it comes to throwing away the paper—in a recycling bin if possible. Buckminster Fuller, internationally known inventor, said, "Pollution is nothing but the resources we are not harvesting. We allow them to disperse because we've been ignorant of their value." That is my eco-lesson for the day. Newspapers are land-based information sheets with day-old information. No offense to my friends in the business (and I might not have any after this chapter), but everything on the page has already happened. And in the case of national newspapers, the human mind cannot possibly absorb the amount of content issued on a daily basis. The pathways of the brain strain under the obligation to read about the murder of a child in detail and then shift to the next story about some pro athlete getting the short end of the stick because he cannot maintain his lifestyle on 25 million bucks. Trying to put all this in some mental order is a surefire way to reach for extra-strength whatever.

So how are things over on the telly? It is estimated that by the time an average child reaches the age of 13, he or she will have witnessed 8,000 murders and over 100,000 other acts of violence on what my mom used to call the "idiot box." By the time that child is 18 years old, he or she will have witnessed 200,000 acts of violence, including 40,000 murders, and because free TV is long gone, we are paying for all this mayhem in more ways than one. So we can all at least consider the possibility that there isn't a whole lot on the tube that moves humanity forward, yes?

Oh yeah, I know, for the most part radio isn't any better. With that in place, I was more than surprised when I was channel surfing (it's much safer than real surfing—no sharks, just teeth-whitening commercials) and came across a show where two women were sitting next to each other. One of them was crying, and the other reminded me of a girl I went to high school with, my drill sergeant in boot camp, the teacher who never let me slack off, and Mary Tyler Moore's straight-talking neighbor Rhoda all rolled into one.

It was, in fact, Rhonda Britten.

Rhonda was raised in Michigan's Upper Peninsula. At the age of 14—when most kids have watched those 8,000 televised murders—she was within arm's length of her parents' murder/suicide—*the real deal*. As you can imagine, the years that followed could best be described as "turbulent" as Rhonda wandered the world not only feeling worthless, but also searching for something that had been ripped apart in an instant—*her soul*. But the farther she ran, the wider the gap became between that traumatized young woman and the person she longed to be. Like all of us, that gap quickly filled up with fear.

Rhonda's transformation from *"fear-full"* to *"fear-less"* did not take place overnight or in some holy instant, but rather over a period of time. Like a seed that takes its time to push through the soil—resting now and then to compose itself before it grows some more—Rhonda finally broke new ground and offered her wisdom to the world. People flocked to her message: *There is life beyond fear.*

It took six months after I first watched Rhonda as one of the co-hosts of the Emmy Award–winning *Starting Over* to get her on my show. She is just a little busy these days, what with writing best-sellers, taping television shows, and traveling the world giving seminars and keynotes. We started our conversation on the air about something Rhonda has become known for the world over—fearless living. It is a role she has accepted, but I am sure would rather not have had to.

"Rhonda, most people don't start out life the way you did, and without getting into all the details, how do you think the death of your parents at such an impressionable age affected you?"

"My father killed my mother and then himself in front of me on Father's Day. When something like that happens, it really doesn't register. You dismiss it, you deny it, you avoid it, and you lie about it—anything but acknowledge it. You basically run away from it. But like everything else, running away just changes the scenery, not the person. So it took a very long time before I was able to see that mostly I was just afraid."

"You know," I said, "it amazes me that fear has so many levels to it. One person's fear is another person's dare. I mean, some people are terrified of flying yet will think nothing of driving a car while eating and talking on a cell phone doing 70 on the interstate. Now that scares me!"

"It's true," Rhonda responded. "Fear is about risk, and things that we perceive as low-risk are not connected to fear. But neither are they connected to human growth in terms of your soul. I have a little chart that I use with people. It looks like a bull's eye, and smack dab in the middle is the *comfort zone*. Life is good there—no fuss, no muss and, for sure, no growth. The first ring outside of the center is the *stretch zone*—something has nudged us out of the comfort zone, and now we have to stretch. Apprehension sets in. You know you are headed for some change and you think it's possible to handle it, but you are not really sure. Fear starts to rear its head, and you take notice. The comfort zone you long for has become a memory. You are having to stretch whether you like it or not. That stretching pushes you into the next ring—the *risk zone*. This is where major growth takes place. Fear has to be confronted and shown for what it is—your *beliefs* about fear. See, fear is just doing what fear does—it cannot be anything different. Love is love, fear is fear, and so forth. Thinking it should be different doesn't make it different; acting in spite of it does."

"Rhonda, how many times does one have to do the bull's-eye thing before we get what's going on?"

"There is no timetable. Some people run through the process a hundred times a day, some one hundred times a year, and others a few hundred times over a lifetime. Much of it depends on the language you use around fear and the ways you either confront it or run from it. And I am here to tell you that running just wears you out. Fear is always right behind you. It's like the neighborhood bully who keeps pushing until you turn around and say 'get lost,' and then he picks on someone else."

"So how does one begin to handle fear—sign up for *Fear Factor?*"

"In some ways, that's not so far off. We have two basic responses: fight or flight. We have already established that fleeing doesn't work too well, so the other option—fighting—is the best way. Of course, the fight is not with someone else; it's within ourselves. I believe that the reason fear is so prevalent is because we don't know that we have a choice."

"What is the other choice?"

"To choose *not* to be afraid. The big ah-ha for me in the years since my parents died was that I finally figured out that the fear was not about me. It was about something that happened, and when we assign fear to events outside of us and then internalize it, the game is on. Then we go looking for people to step in and rescue us, save us or exempt us from our fears. And you know what, John? That is never going to happen because they cannot take away what you put there."

Wow.

I asked, "What about that old adage, 'Fear knocked on the door, faith answered, and no one was there'? Does that work for you?"

"Look, I know what worked for me, and since fear is equal in its ability to paralyze everybody, I am very confident when I say that faith without action is not faith. It's just more fear. Action is movement, and you don't move if you don't have faith. So faith can be an important ally, but if all you do is talk it and not walk it, nothing will change."

"Rhonda, day after day we are bombarded with every known news story about all the reasons we have to be afraid, from terrorists to some new disease to something that you were a witness to—murder. You have a different perspective than most of us when it comes to at least one of these events, and I am clear on the fact that people who have experienced something the rest of us only see but have never been involved in are much more experienced in how to handle the fallout. What language should we use surrounding the fears we have? I mean, can we talk ourselves into it and, if so, then out of it?"

"Excellent question, John. If you are honest with yourself, you will know you are afraid of something. You start making excuses: *I could have done that but . . . I should have done that but . . . If it wasn't for my parents, I would have . . . If my boss would just, then I would . . . If someone would just come along and make everything better, then I would . . . could . . . should . . .* You know the drill. It's like that old movie line: *I could have been a contender!* The deal is that all those things you think should change so you can move back into your comfort zone are not going to change, period. The only person on the entire planet you really have any leverage on is yourself, and if you don't have any yet, you need to get some. We attract what we think we deserve, so if you go through life feeling worthless because of something that happened 40 years ago, you will continue to get more of the same."

"So, do we have to get on the couch, go back in time and try to figure out where things went wrong?"

"Not unless you want to relive everything over and over again, hoping that you will feel different this time around. You can never go back and fill in all the holes, but you can start from this moment, make new choices, and find a new path to your life that is not fear-driven. I will never understand why my father killed my mother and then himself— never in a million years. I can come up with theories and ideas, and none of those will change the actions he took. But I can change the actions *I* take, and that is far more important when it comes to living our lives at a level of confidence and trust in ourselves."

Wow . . . again. But she wasn't finished quite yet.

"Most people I have worked with over the years seem to be waiting for someone or something outside of themselves for permission to move on. Years go by, and we wait . . . and wait . . . and wait. Nothing happens, and do you know why? Because not only is no one coming, but also you wouldn't believe them if they did grant you permission to live your life in spite of fear. How many people do you know, including yourself, who keep doing the same things over and over again, hurting themselves and the people around them, and they know it on some level, but continue to do it anyway? It's because they have not gotten to the point inside where the person they should trust the most—themselves—gives them permission to drop what was and move on to what can be. Look, this is tough stuff for sure, and it's not going to be easy. Life is not set up to be easy. Only humans think this way, and it holds us back. Growth is a constant wrestling match between who we think we are—based on our beliefs—and who we hope to become some day. If fear is the deciding factor, guess what wins out every time?"

By the time you read this, Rhonda will have returned to the high school she graduated from—the same community that witnessed a 14-year-old girl's tragedy so many years ago—to deliver the commencement address to a group of young people getting ready to take on the world. But she will not be returning as the person she was, but rather as the person she was capable of becoming. The best-selling author of *Fearless Living*, founder of the Fearless Living Institute, and Emmy Award–winning and nationally recognized life coach will have shared a very important lesson with the future doctors, lawyers, business owners, authors, teachers, truck drivers, and parents in attendance.

"You can either let your circumstances define you, or you can rise above the fear and confusion to create a life that has meaning, respect, and integrity as its guideposts. How you choose to see your life will be the life you experience from this day forward. Don't just look to the future, but also within yourselves, for the truth resides there. It's your job to bring forth your light in a world that appears to be very dark with fear and illuminate the way for those to follow."

Light those torches, folks. We have work to do.

Complaining just advertises your fears to the world, and the last thing you want to do is feed fear in any way, shape, or form. In order to live a fearless life, you have to know the truth—that there is nothing wrong with you. Fear is the culprit, and once exposed for what it is, the only thing that can get in the way of the life you want to lead is you.

—Rhonda Britten

Freedom from Fear

I took a refresher course in human development not too long ago. I had first attended it 20 years ago, and after three days of looking at the things that had built up over the years and once again held me back from experiencing a greater level of awareness and service in my life (and no, I am not going to tell you what they were—that's my business!), the group was put through something called "The Danger Process." Of course, there was much apprehension about what that would entail, and you could actually feel the fear mounting in the room, even though we were all safe in a well-lit and stationary brick building—no terrorists, no ax murderers, no IRS agents, no drunk drivers, or bungee cords. You could see the look of fear in people's eyes because uncertainty lay ahead.

I promised not to talk about how the process is performed, but let's just say that when it was all said and done, we all knew that the two biggest things we fear are each other and ourselves. In a world that is getting increasingly smaller and putting us in closer contact with each other, that's not a good sign. In a day and age where what we used to do to "fix" our lives doesn't work too well anymore and leaves us with only one place left to go—within—we had better begin to address the fears in us that keep us on the sidelines of life before the game is over. Fear has the same consistency as faith. Matter of fact, both of them exist only because we make them so. And so our lives depend on which one we choose to lean on when the going gets tough, because if it hasn't already, it certainly will.

Rhonda Britten experienced an event that could have forever bound her in the chains of fear, but she chose to keep testing the steel that seemed so real until one day her constraints gave way to the truth and something that FDR told us in one of our darkest hours: *The only thing we have to fear is fear itself.*

Get a Grip

There are some things you should be fearful of. Opening a box of Cracker Jack and not finding a prize inside. Sitting in a barber's chair and hearing, "How short did you say?" Perhaps even swimming in the open ocean with a deep laceration in your leg and a sign around your neck that says "LUNCH" on it. Humans have been around for thousands of years, and we have been afraid of everything from thunderstorms sent by angry gods to diseases that were supposed to wipe us out—and never did. It's time to get a grip. Have confidence in your ability to overcome the latest round of pestilence and doomsayers letting you know that it's all about to end. I cannot imagine too many things more terrifying to a young girl than watching her father die by his own hand right in front of her after taking the life of her mother. That event created fear. No one would deny it, but Rhonda was able to overcome it. So instead of yakking about everything that is going wrong in the world, find one thing that is good in your life and celebrate it. Share it and watch it expand.

Realize It's Not Real

One summer night in 1967, my dad took the family to a drive-in theater. My next-door neighbor Vinny was with us, and it wasn't until after the cartoons were over and it was dark enough to see the screen did we realize that sitting in front of the car on lawn chairs—outside the safety of the back seat—was not a good idea. It was the outdoor premiere of *Night of the Living Dead,* and by the time it was over, the two of us were stuck together like 10-year-old Silly Putty. That night on the sleepover, we lay in bed back-to-back, covers up to our eyes, filled with fear and sure that some ghoul or zombie was about to break in and eat our brains. The fear *felt* real, but it was simply a reaction to what we *thought* was real. Fear does that because we allow it to.

Here is a quick way to find out if there are any zombies that need to be removed in your closet. On a sheet of paper, write down everything you are afraid of. Next to each item write "real" or "imagined." Now, here is the kicker: it's the same thing. *You have to imagine it in order for it to be real,* and *for it to be real, you have to imagine it.* Fear then only means what you think it means . . . and nothing more.

Turn Around

Fear is a lot like love—and faith and joy and sadness and every other human emotion. It gathers energy like a snowball rolling downhill unless you stop it in its tracks. Much like the schoolyard bully or the blowhard in the bar, the best thing you can do to diffuse the energy is turn around and get in its hip pocket.

Many moons ago, I worked as a security guard on third shift at a major Chicago hotel. One time, I was called to a room only to find a naked woman in the hallway crying profusely. I gave her my jacket and entered the room to find a guy sitting on the bed, totally out of his mind and with his hand under the blanket. He began to withdraw his hand, and I yelled, "If you pull that gun out, it's going to look awful funny sticking out of (a certain orifice of the human body)." Was I afraid? You bet. I was filled with fear, absolutely, but in a split second I decided that my fear was based on the uncertainty of what might happen. And if I was certain in the face of uncertainty, I could overcome it. The guy froze, not knowing what to do, and I moved forward. We "chatted" (really close together) until the law showed up. It turned out the guy had just been released from prison, and he held a 9-mm semi-automatic with a full clip. It was also my last day on the job. If something is causing you fear, turn around and move toward it. You might be surprised at how quickly it disappears or becomes something else. Be certain in the face of uncertainty.

Buy a Cape

I dare you to get a one-piece suit with a big F on the front for FEAR-LESS. Do you know that more than 95 percent of the things we fear never happen? And the remaining 5 percent might just be happening because we believe it. Just for one day, pretend you are the superhero of your choosing—Superman, Wonder Woman, Aquaman, Green Hornet, Batgirl, whoever. (You don't have to tell anyone unless you want to.) Did you ever notice that superheroes thrive on fear, but move forward in spite of it? Superheroes don't waste time being fearful of little things like people not liking them, what kind of clothes they are wearing (obviously), and the neighbor they think is a spy. Real-life issues require bigger-than-life answers, and coming from the perspective of Clark Kent might work better for you than Joe or Jane Average. But if this is asking too much, go rent *Superman* and pay attention. Oh yeah, no jumping off buildings. But if you do climb the nearest corporate skyscraper and you see a guy shooting webs out of his wrists, it might not be Peter Parker. ... It could be me.

Cut It Off

For some people, the only basis for their identity is fear. They are not sure what they are afraid of, but they know something is stalking them ... getting closer ... and closer. With the combination of the media bringing every horrible story right into our living rooms, the talk-radio hosts blathering about how evil the other political party is, and the newspapers reporting on the downfall of civilization from every angle, it's no wonder that we live in a perpetual state of fear. (Remember, uncertainty is the breeding ground for fear.) So here is what you do.

First, the last thing you should download into your consciousness before you try to sleep is the news. Turn it off. Watch reruns of *Saturday Night Live* or some old movie (not *Night of the Living Dead*), read or talk with your significant other, sit on the porch, or color or draw. But cut the umbilical cord of fear before you sleep.

Second, guard what conversations you engage in during the day. We have somehow confused talking with doing in America, and they are not the same things. Advertising your fears, as Rhonda points out, is a sure way to keep them alive. Nip it in the bud. You are better off talking about the latest celebrity screw-up instead of the fear that permeates so much of today's conversations.

Finally, get this: no one is exempt from the tragedies of life. For all the privilege that the Kennedy's have enjoyed, there is no way I would trade places with any of those folks. Your life will have its moments that bring you to your knees in fear, but faith will lift you up again. Rhonda Britten is an example of what is possible for each of us, no matter what comes our way. Chalk one up for fearless living.

CHAPTER 18

Love Lights the Way

There is no guarantee that love will add years to your life, but it will most certainly add life to your years.

—John St.Augustine

The range of human emotions is far-reaching, and I have always been interested in observing them. We are ruled by our emotions and our emotional responses to the world we see and the people we meet. Of all the emotions we can feel, love is, of course, the most celebrated the world over. Everyone is looking for it, giving it, or hoping for it. I can't think of any other emotion that comes with so many attachments. Unconditional love is a concept that we talk about, but few, except the young and pets, seem to understand and display it. Maybe someday we will learn that love cannot survive with conditions and restrictions placed on it.

The two most noted events in our lives are when we enter and exit. I prefer to think that a timetable somewhere dictates our movements, and that we come in on time and go out on time, even though it may not seem like it to the world at large. The lesson theme these two events carry is the same: love.

When we celebrate the birth of a child, an incredible outpouring of hope and love is put forth for this little human who has arrived, no matter the circumstances surrounding the birth. When we are present at a funeral or memorial, there is an equal outpouring of hope and love as well—the love we have for those who have gone ahead of us and the hope that this time we won't forget what a precious gift life really is.

Whatever way you look at it, love is the energy that infuses the human spirit with the very stuff we are made of. Without it, well, just turn on the news to see what happens when we forget what love is all about.

Agape is the giving, nondemanding side of love. It is being concerned for the life and growth of those who are close to us—the type of love that is displayed by a parent for a child. Agape is an unconditional validation of another human being and is a Greek word for spiritual love. *Philos* is the love found in long-term friendships. It is also the feeling of love that Jesus invoked us to display: "Love thy neighbor as thyself." If you were to put these two powerful emotions into other words, they would spell Chelsey Jo Hewitt, Timothy Wotchko, and Jerry Collins—three young people who taught an entire community about the transcending and transformational power of love.

On February 26, 2002, I was getting ready to head home after putting the lid on another three hours of radio. I sat as I always do after the show, letting the energy slowly drain off my body and brain as I gazed out the window. The snow was really coming down hard. My thoughts went back eight years to when I sat in the hospital room with my daughter Amanda, who had just gone through having her kidney removed at age 5. The same kind of weather had surrounded us then, and I thought about how many days and hours had passed since that time. The ringing phone snapped me out of my trance. It was my son Andy telling me to be careful on the drive home because the weather was really bad.

When Old Man Winter does his thing in Upper Michigan, he does not fool around. This night was no exception. I crawled along the roads in my truck and was relieved to see the porch light of home. As my family and I started talking about the day, the phone rang. My producer, Ann Marie, told me that there had been a terrible accident in the next town. They thought there were a few kids in the car, and that one of the kids might be Chelsey Hewitt. I had met Chelsey a couple of times, and her parents Doug and Robin had attended some of my live events. The thought shot through me that I had just talked with Chelsey the night before at a basketball game. She had rushed up to me with her friend Liz Kinnart and was lit up like a Christmas tree—she had gotten her driver's license that very day.

By the time I made it to the Kinnarts' home, the scene was overwhelming. Chelsey and her boyfriend Tim Wotchko had been hit broadside by a semi trailer truck on their way to school where Chelsey was to sing the National Anthem before a basketball game. Sixteen-year-old Chelsey died instantly. Tim, age 17, had been transported to Wisconsin in critical condition. Teenagers filled the house with their tears and grief. It was without a doubt the saddest experience of their lives. In one moment, boys became men and girls became women out of the loss of their friends and love for one another. I found out that when the officers came on the accident scene, they were astonished to see the kids without a mark on them. Chelsey's head rested on Tim's chest, and when she was moved, he took a breath. There was still hope, but the morning after brought no comfort. Tim died from his injuries. Incredibly, as if he had known what lay ahead, he had told his mom only a week prior that he wanted to be an organ donor. Because of his wishes, a half-dozen other people had a new chance at life the night Tim Wotchko made his transition. It amazes me that one so young understood the power in giving life by being an organ donor. Just like money (you can't take it with you), our collective unwillingness to give a part of ourselves after our time is over amazes me.

The next day, we cancelled all guests for the radio show and started out what I thought would be a short tribute to these two remarkable kids. Liz Kinnart and Danny Larrabee (a classmate of Tim's) came into the studio, and we opened the phone lines for anyone who wanted to express their feelings. What started out as a one-hour segment lasted four and a half hours as people who knew them—and many who did not—called in to express their grief and sorrow and to sing their praises. We heard from neighbors, family, classmates, and one man who called in and spoke in a breaking voice about his brother who had died nearly 40 years ago in a car accident. I truly could have stopped doing radio after that show and been satisfied that the medium was being used for the highest good. As tragic as the incident was, on some level a healing took place during those few hours on the air.

As one might imagine, the wakes and funerals for Chelsey and Tim strained the confines of the funeral homes and churches as mourners stood in line to pay their respects to Doug and Robin, and Tim's parents, Dennis and Kathy. At each wake, the parents greeted countless tears with smiles, so thankful that their children had had such an impact on so many people in such a short time. Stories were shared about Tim's dedication to spending time with the younger kids, teaching them basketball skills for an hour after his practice had ended. One of those younger boys is my son Andy, who stood at Tim's casket and sobbed, "Who is going to teach me to shoot free throws now, Dad?" It was one of those times in which no words could ease the pain.

Chelsey was remembered for being the girl everyone came to for advice. She was a mender of fences—so easily broken in high school—and was a popular cheerleader and friend to even the kids no one else talked to. She loved to sing and made sure that the color pink was part of every wardrobe and in every corner of her life. She was remembered for treating other people the way she wanted to be treated, with dignity, integrity, and love. Her classmates held each other up as they said good-bye to a lifelong friend.

The night Chelsey's wake ended, a basketball game was scheduled at the high school Tim attended and played for. Jerry Collins, the varsity coach, asked me if I would say a few words in the locker room to the team before the game.

I couldn't think of much to say, but I did the best I could. "Fellas, you have just learned that life is a very precious thing. Every moment counts, and there are no guarantees. You all knew Tim a lot better than I did, so just take a minute to think of something he taught you. If you do that—and live that lesson every day—then Tim will remain with you as long as you live." I stood with my right hand on Jerry Collins' shoulder as one of the boys spoke up. "Tim always said that you do something 100 percent or you don't do it at all." The team quickly agreed that lesson would become Tim's legacy, and they would do what they could to live up to it. Tears streamed down Jerry's face and ran into the big smile that went from ear to ear. The boys went out into the gym to thunderous applause. The wound had begun to heal over, but it would be short-lived.

Eight months later, on October 2, Jerry Collins died in an auto accident. He was 25 years old. Certain levels of grief cannot even begin to be calibrated—pain so deep that it seems to transcend the physical aspects of life and love so powerful that it can only be fully revealed by death.

Jerry's death, so closely linked to Chelsey and Tim's passing just months before, took on an almost prophetic tone. Just a week before he died, Jerry had told a friend over pizza. "If I died tomorrow, it would be all right. Coaching basketball and working with the boys has been a dream come true." One week later, he was gone.

How many of us could say the same thing ... and mean it?

All lessons (especially the ones we don't like) are repeated until an understanding allows for further instruction—perhaps a greater awareness. In the four years since Chelsey, Tim, and Jerry left, the changes in the lives of their families—brought about by their absence—have been profound and private, as they should be. But the messages for the rest of us who knew the kids—and for those of you who have just met them on these pages—are clear.

There is no guarantee that you are going to be here tomorrow, much less next week or next year. If you don't give 100 percent of your effort and focus to your life, what is the point in being here? If you are not about treating other people the way you want to be treated, what is the point of being here? If you cannot say that your life is the dream that you always wanted it to be, and that if you died tomorrow it would be all right because you knew you had fulfilled your destiny, what is the point of being here?

Let me spell it out for you. The point of being here is to live your dreams as if your life depends on it—because it does. Each of us fills a niche so unique, so vital, that to live any other way is in direct conflict with the laws of Spirit. Chelsey Jo Hewitt was the only person who could wear pink that way. It was more than a color; it was her faith. She was the only one who could sing the National Anthem with that voice. She was the only person in the world who could have possibly gone up to the girl to whom no one else paid attention and, through a wink and a smile, made her feel that she mattered. Chelsey was the only one who could say, "What's important in life is how we treat each other"—and mean it. At the age of 16, she already understood what millions of people in counseling are still trying to figure out. Chelsey knew who she was, what she stood for, and where she was going. Do you?

Timothy J. Wotchko may have died in an auto accident, but because he did things 100 percent or not at all, he still lives on today. Somewhere in the Midwest, Tim's heart beats for a woman who would have died if not for his vision. A man who needed a liver transplant was given a second chance at life. Tim's kidneys filter the blood of someone who had been connected to dialysis and can now enjoy time with her granddaughter. Tim knew that he was part of everyone—just as we all are, but so often forget. And he proved it by telling his mother that if anything should happen, he wanted to live on. He gave his attention and energy to a whole class of boys by taking time to show them how to shoot a free throw and spin a ball on their finger. Those boys are nearing Tim's age now, and I have no doubt that he is never far away from their thoughts. Timmy knew who he was, what he stood for, and where he was going—at the age of 17. Do you?

Gerald "Jerry" Lee Collins was wise beyond his years. He knew that attitude was more important than aptitude. Basketball was a way for him to develop leadership, teamwork, and the lessons that come with winning and losing. While he was "The Coach," he was also a friend to dozens of young men who needed someone to fill the role of mentor. He understood their language, knew their problems, and, most importantly, walked his talk. He was an example of how young people should view their lives—as opportunities to live their dreams, to touch others, and to be so happy that even the thought of death cannot dampen the passion of being alive. "If I died tomorrow, it wouldn't matter because I am happy with my life." At 25, Jerry knew who he was, what he stood for, and where he was going. I am guessing you know the question that belongs here now.

The passing of these three young lives stopped time for hundreds of people, making us look at and listen to who we truly are. John Lennon said, "All you need is love," but in what form? From whom? As defined by what? Love has many forms, and the word is thrown around on many levels. In an instant, three lives were born into eternity, and hundreds of others became like one through the fusion of love—the ability of this unseen force to meld the differences we have into a common bond.

These three amazing teachers held class once again. Death's greatest lesson is to love life. No one reading this book has a stamped guarantee on how long they will be here. If you get nothing else from this book, get this: love of self is a most difficult life lesson. You will never feel the love you seek from others if you are not accepting of who you are—and can love yourself with all your faults, talents, shortcomings, and "long goings." You can love your house, your job, your car, and your new shoes, but in reality your love of these "things" is nothing more than who you are in relation to them—how you feel when you put on those new shoes or how you see yourself in the new car or job. Your outer world reflects your inner world. Take a look at your life and the things in it. Now take a look at the people in your life. Which reflection is the strongest? What have you bought into your life and why? Who have you brought into your life and why?

Some of the most watched shows on television are about connecting with "the other side." People are desperate to know that their loved ones have crossed the threshold of death and that they are well and did not suffer. I am fascinated with our fascination with contacting those who have gone before us. As I watch these shows go through the motions of connecting with the dearly departed and help bring closure or enlightenment or whatever to the living, it dawns on me why people flock to this type of thing: guilt. At the risk of making a blanket statement—and, certainly, there are exceptions—most of us are too busy to really connect with the people in our lives until it's too late. Or we spend our very precious little time on Earth majoring in minor things with those close to us. Then, when the bell sounds the death knell, we seek out ways to know that the dearly departed are all right or that we are forgiven for some transgression—one that we most likely had the opportunity to clear up in person, but did not do so.

Death has a way of bringing forth what is important. No doubt, it's a shock to lose a child or a spouse or a parent—and finding some type of relief is good for the soul. But it is also good for the soul to take the moments we have and make the most of them. It is the ultimate lesson offered to us by Chelsey, Tim, and Jerry.

Do things 100 percent or don't do them at all.

—Timothy J. Wotchko

If I died tomorrow, it would be OK ... because I am happy with my life.

—Gerald Lee Collins

What's important in life is how we treat each other.

—Chelsey Jo Hewitt

Love Matters Most

If only I had more love in my life ... If only more people loved me ...
If only I could be loved for who I really am ... If only love didn't hurt
so much ... I would just love to have thinner thighs ... I really would
love to have a better job ... I absolutely love my kids ... Love means
never having to say you're sorry ... *The Love Boat* ... exciting and new
... The Love Shack, baby ... *Love Story* ... Love's theme ... The power
of love ... Love can build a bridge ... Love the one you're with ... We
love hunting ... swimming ... golf ... tennis ... fishing ... TV ...
NASCAR ... bowling ... gardening ... our pets ... our cars ... our
iPod ... our remote control ... nature ... the Cubs (until September)
... sports idols ... and, of course, ... money.

I have omitted the 9 billion other "things" we love due to space
constrictions. But, hopefully, you get the drift.

Love in its clearest essence is the feeling we get when someone
close to us dies because that force is our connection to them. Their
absence from our lives gives us a sense of priority that is usually

embedded among the minutiae of life. The love that poured forth when Chelsey, Tim, and Jerry died created a ripple effect. People who did not even know them recognized what had been missing from their own existence—the three lessons of love. First, treating others as we should treat ourselves, with pride, dignity, and respect. Second, living your life to the fullest—a 100 percent commitment to stop whining about your life and creating an existence that leads to the third lesson of love: a purpose that transcends our own little piece of dirt and touches the lives of others. It's about keeping the essence of who we are—love—alive forever.

It's been said that that which hurts, instructs. Humans by design are forgetful creatures. Death by design is a powerful reminder. Come from a place of love, and you will be sure to inspire before you expire. Following the lead of three amazing young people, consider the suggestions below.

Write Your Own Obituary

Sounds gruesome, but someone's going to do it sooner or later. Much like Ebenezer Scrooge, you still have time to make a change—but not until you recognize what needs to change. I have reminded you quite a few times in this book that "when in doubt, write it out." Considering that many people are in doubt as to what their lives mean or stand for—who they are, where they are going, and what it all means—sitting down to put in print how your life will look at the end might just save it in the middle. Open up the newspaper and read some of the obits, both famous and unknown. People are doing incredible things with their lives. Are you one of them?

Sit in a Cemetery

When I walked to Chicago in 1996, my companions and I stopped at a small cemetery near Brookside, Wisconsin. Wandering through the rows of headstones—some dating back 150 years, some only weeks old—was a very humbling experience. As I noticed the ages on many of them from the last century, I realized that so often they had passed away in their teenage years. Some had made it to their 40s, yet still before it should have been their time. Any time that you have left—that they did not—is gravy as far as I am concerned. Once your name is etched in stone, there are no second chances to make that phone call, no more opportunities to say you're sorry, no more days to hold a hand or buy an ice cream or watch the sunrise. Your time is gone. How much time do you have left to really live?

Make the Connection

The world fell in love with an alien in the movie, *E.T.* The little frog-looking creature "turned on his heart light" and promised Elliott that "I will always be here" as he touched his chest, while the organ inside glowed with love. The world is filled with people who could use some of your good energy, which is always replenished when used with great intent. Too many of us have turned off the "heart light" and put up a "no vacancy sign" on our love energy, most likely because we've been hurt once or even five times. But by extending yourself once again when it comes to love, you are really expanding yourself.

Give All You Can

Here is a great way to keep your perspective, focus, and priorities in order. Buy a good-sized hourglass and keep it where you can see it. Give it a tip, and in 60 seconds the sand will have drained from the top to the bottom. In that time span, 18 people died due to a domestic injury of some kind, six people died in an auto accident, and 11 people died in hospitals from misdiagnoses. For every second, minute, hour, and day that we hold ourselves back from giving and receiving the love we need to function, we are losing slices of time we can ill afford to lose. Make the call, hold the hand, give the hug—and do it to 100 percent of your capacity and capability.

Love Your Life

It's been my experience that people who love being alive differ from those who think that somehow life is a burden because of one main ingredient—purpose. People who know why they are here like being here. People who have no idea what the heck is going on feel like they are in prison. Your get-out-of-jail-free card is to stop running on the treadmill and get quiet. Most of humanity's problems come from our unwillingness to sit alone in a room for more than five minutes and listen for the "still, small voice." For me, it took walking to Chicago and back to Michigan to "get it." For you, it might just be sitting in your car in the parking lot—without the radio blasting—and simply being quiet. And consider that you might already be living your purpose and not even know it. We are always presented with choices in life. If we choose with love and respect for ourselves and those around us, the sun shines a bit brighter. If we choose from a place of lack, fear, or pain, it gets pretty dark. The world seems to be a place in need of a few more floodlights, and if you are not too busy, you might consider shining your inner light just a little brighter. You never know how far it will go or who will need it. On behalf of the rest of humanity, we would really appreciate it.

CHAPTER 19

It's About Time

How vain it is to sit down to write when you
have not stood up to live.

—Henry David Thoreau

W
hen I first read that quote many years ago, I vowed that I would never just put thoughts or recycled theory on paper to further some agenda or concept. It's my observation that the bookshelves are lined with volumes from so many of today's talking heads *who know everything about everything, but haven't done anything.* They rely heavily on examples rather than experience.

It's been five years since the idea for *Living an Uncommon Life* presented itself to me. I wasn't fully ready to write it at that time. I still had more moments to experience in order to offer the most complete blueprint as the scribe of this work. As you know by now, during that time, I left the world of radio even though I had enjoyed so much success and satisfaction. It was an agonizing decision, and I could not fully comprehend the purpose at the time. It was only when my father passed away just over a year later that I understood that my decision was intended for him and me to spend time together in the last months of his life. It was a healing time for both of us, one that many people never get the opportunity to experience. During our time together, old trespasses were forgotten, and laughter took their place. Instead of seeing the gulf between us, I was amazed to find the similarities. What I used to think were boxes of junk collected over many years became valuable and priceless memories as we sat together on the porch of my sister's home, and he told me the story behind every key chain, tie tack, bowling award, and picture of my mother, who died in 1997.

Something happens to a man when his father dies. For me, it was akin to being in an assembly line and suddenly moving to the front of the line. Some of the little boy in me disappeared, and the special times shared between dad and son will be forever sealed away in my memory because there is no longer anyone to relate them to, no one to share them with. I have begun to feel for the first time in my life that I am in the position to have more yesterdays than tomorrows. After burying my father's ashes along with my mom's at the grave of her parents in a small Navarino, Wisconsin, cemetery, I knew it was time to begin writing in earnest. My father's passing reminded me, first and foremost, that each moment—whether filled with pain or pleasure, scarcity or abundance, laughter or tears—is irreplaceable, and that our lives are really nothing more than a series of moments, held together by the thoughts, dreams, and desires that make up the grand illusion each of us chooses to create and experience for a very brief time.

When the transformation within me was completed for this particular cycle, I emerged from my self-induced cocoon to see where my newly sprouted wings would take me. The first stop on my journey was back to the radio dial. Thirty-three months away had given me a new sense of urgency to convey my message, but the maturation process made the delivery of that message much more exact, as well as passionate. While I am no less distressed about what goes on in the world—how poorly we treat each other and ourselves—I am more confident in what I can be in relation to the challenges. I know I have more to offer now in the way of perspective on issues that have seemingly plagued humanity forever.

The second stop on my journey is this book you hold in your hands. I spent countless days and nights sitting in front of the computer screen, perusing notes inscribed on everything from paper to napkins to the palm of my hand. Hour after hour, I listened to old radio shows with the people you have read about in this work, even spending time with a few who did not make full mention here, but whose message was needed on that particular day to add to the impact of a chapter. The late Christopher Reeve talked about his spiritual growth as a by-product of the love between him and his wife Dana, who has also gone ahead. Senator Paul Simon of Illinois, who died in 2003, remarked that the most important thing to remember is that you cannot legislate moral behavior, but you can legislate with a moral compass. My late friend Percy Ross, who gave millions away during his life to those in need, helped to raise money on the air for a woman he never met whose house had burned to the ground. To hear their voices after they have gone reminded me that, while our own voices will one day be silent, who we are lives on.

Contrary to what the Rolling Stones would tell you, time is *not* on your side. It's moving forward every second, separating you from the past and thrusting you into the future. How you move into whatever time you have left is your choice. What you do is a direct result of who you believe yourself to be. Your voice matters in things great and small. If you allow yourself to get out of the way, the way will be shown. If you live the truth as best you know it, the consequences will be of your choosing and not someone else's. Being responsible for your actions is a sure way to reclaim your power. Letting go of the things you thought defined you for the opportunity to be defined by something much greater than you brings with it a sense of purpose that no material thing can match.

About 2,600 years ago, Socrates sealed his fate by telling people that "the unexamined life is not worth living." After a few mock trials and a cup of hemlock, early Greece's version of Dr. Phil was toast because he spoke the truth, as he knew it. We all know it, but few of us actually stop long enough to take an objective view of our existence and make some sense out of the senseless moments in which we have participated. While the unexamined life is not worth living, *the uncommon life is worth everything.*

While this book features some truly amazing people, it's not about them. It's about *you.* It's about the choices you make, the thoughts you think, the words you say, and the deeds you do. No matter how low things may look at this stage of your life, know that flight is assured in the end to all who seek it.

Catherine Crier passed along a Buddhist saying to me a few years ago that goes something like this: *He who knows and does not act never really knows.* We live in a time that gives us access to technology that no other humans in history have had. We live in a time of more opportunity, more abundance, and more possibility than anyone who has come before us. Who we become in relation to this information will determine the world we live in. What we do with what we know will clear the path for generations that will follow. It begins and ends with each of us.

Be the change.

One Voice

In these days of torment and strain upon our hearts,
When darkness seems so close to us, and living really hurts,
Upon the rocks of life and in the sound of screams,
There's always been a bit of hope, and it's the voice of dreams.
It's just one voice in the stillness of the night,
Speaking for the children and listening for their cries.
It's just the voice of a child who dreams of better days,
The faithful sound of all of us in peace and hope and praise.
It may seem that God's deserted us and left us on our own,
Taken back a promise and closed the doors to home,
All alone to struggle with the conflict and the pain,
Searching for the sunshine in the midst of all this rain.
It's just one voice in the darkest part of night,
Praying for the children and listening for their sighs.
It's just the voice of a man who dreams of better days,
Ringing through the universe in peace and hope and praise.
And when the storms have passed, and the pain has gone away
The love and light of children gives birth to a brand-new day.
When the prayers of all the ages bring your dreams to you,
Know that it's your voice that God has listened to.
It's just one voice, in the stillness of the night,
Singing for the children and looking for the light.
It's just one voice, one that speaks the truth,
The one true voice in all the world is the one that lives in you.

—John St.Augustine

RECOMMENDED
Resources

John Denver
Online . . .
About JD: www.johndenver.com
Plant-It 2020—Planting Trees Worldwide: www.plantit2020.org
The Windstar Foundation: www.wstar.org
Listen to . . .
An Evening with John Denver—CD
The Harbor Lights Concert—CD
Watch . . .
The Wildlife Concert—DVD
Let This Be a Voice—DVD

James Amos Jr.
Read . . .
Focus or Failure: America at the Crossroads
The Memorial: A Novel of the Vietnam War
The Complete Idiots Guide to Franchising

Cheryl Richardson
Online . . .
About Cheryl: www.cherylrichardson.com

Read ...
Take Time for Your Life
Life Makeovers
Stand Up for Your Life
The Unmistakable Touch of Grace

Wayne Dyer

Online ...
About Wayne: www.drwaynedyer.com
Read ...
Real Magic: Creating Miracles in Everyday Life
Wisdom of the Ages: A Modern Master Brings Everyday Truths into Everyday Life
Inspiration: Your Ultimate Calling
Listen to ...
The Power of Intention—Audio

Walter Payton

Online ...
The Walter and Connie Payton Foundation: www.payton34.com
Read and watch ...
Payton—Book w/DVD
Pure Payton—DVD
Never Die Easy

Bill Kurtis

Online ...
About Bill: The Arts and Entertainment Network—www.aetv.com
Bill's Country: www.theredbuffalo.com
Bill's Beef: www.tallgrassbeef.com
Read ...
The Death Penalty on Trial: Crisis in American Justice
Forever Kansas!
Watch ...
Cold Case Files, Investigative Reports, American Justice, The A&E Network

Jerry Kramer

Online ...
About Jerry: www.jerrykramer.com
Read ...
Instant Replay (with Dick Schaap)
Distant Replay (with Dick Schaap)
Farewell to Football
Instant Replay (2006 Edition)
Listen to ...
Inside the Locker Room—CDs

Oprah Winfrey

Online ...
About Oprah: www.oprah.com
Read ...
O, The Oprah Magazine
Watch ...
The Oprah Winfrey Show
Oprah After the Show, Oxygen Network

The Road Warriors

Online ...
About Animal and Hawk: www.roadwarriorsinc.com
Watch ...
The Life and Death of the Road Warriors—Double DVD Set
Contact ...
Joe Laurinaitis for speaking engagements: www.roadwarriorsinc.com

Dorothy Hamill

Online ...
About Dorothy: www.dorothyhamill.com
Read ...
On and Off the Ice
Watch ...
Skating with Celebrities, FOX

Jerry Coffee

Online . . .
About Jerry: www.captaincoffee.com
Read . . .
Beyond Survival
Listen to . . .
Beyond Survival—Audio
Watch . . .
Beyond Survival—Video

Dr. Kathleen Hall

Online . . .
About Kathleen: www.drkathleenhall.com
Read . . .
A Life in Balance
Alter Your Life

Earl Hamner

Online . . .
About Earl: www.the-waltons.com
Read . . .
Spencer's Mountain
The Avocado Drive Zoo
Earl Hamner: From Walton's Mountain to Tomorrow by James E. Person, Jr.
Watch . . .
The Waltons

Maureen Moss

Online . . .
About Maureen: www.maureenmoss.com
Read . . .
The Nature of Bliss
Commitment to Love
Listen to . . .
The Nature of Bliss—CD

Hal Thau

Online . . .
Almost Heaven: John Denver's America: www.johndenver.com
Read . . .
Bronx to Broadway: A Life in Show Business

Rhonda Britten

Online . . .
About Rhonda: www.fearlessliving.org
Read . . .
Fearless Living
Change Your Life in 30 Days
Do I Look Fat in This?
Watch . . .
Starting Over

Chelsey Jo Hewitt, Timothy Wotchko, Jerry Collins

Online . . .
Auto safety: www.crashproofyourkids.com
Read . . .
Crash Proof Your Kids: Make Your Teen a Smarter, Safer Driver
  by Timothy Smith
Remember . . .
Tell your kids how important they are to you and the goal is to
  arrive alive.

Catherine Crier

Online . . .
About Catherine: www.criercommunications.com
Read . . .
The Case Against Lawyers
Contempt: How the Right Is Wronging American Justice
Watch . . .
Catherine Crier Live, CourtTV

John St.Augustine

Online . . .
About John: www.johnstaugustine.com
Read . . .
The Tao of Pooh by Benjamin Hoff
The Road Less Traveled by M. Scott Peck
The Success Principles by Jack Canfield
Listen to . . .
Still Me by Christopher Reeve (audio book)
Hesselville by David Stoddard: www.davidstoddard.com
Wind Beneath My Wings by Cathy Bolton: www.cathybolton.com
Watch . . .
The Seven Faces of Dr. Lao
Mr. Smith Goes to Washington
Oh, God!

About the Author

John St.Augustine has been called "a powerful voice of change" by veteran broadcaster Bill Kurtis and "the most influential voice on radio" by best-selling author Cheryl Richardson. His daily show used common sense to define common issues to create an uncommon life experience. He is also the creator of the one-minute vignette "Powerthoughts!," which have inspired thousands of listeners nationwide through his decade-long, award-winning, Michigan-based talk radio show. He is a three-time recipient of the Best Talk Radio Show award from the Michigan Association of Broadcasters. Since the inception of his show in 1997, he has broadcast more than 8,000 programs and interviewed more than 5,000 people from all walks of life. Currently, he is a producer at Harpo Radio for the "Oprah & Friends" channel on XM Satellite Radio.

While St.Augustine is proud of his many media awards and accolades, he cites his 2002 kidney donation to his daughter Amanda as his greatest achievement. St.Augustine is also a sought-after speaker on human potential and purpose, an inspirational and a gifted communicator who has presented his message of hope and possibility to more than 500,000 people via his keynotes and "Lifeworks!" seminars. A native of Chicago, he now lives with his family in Michigan's Upper Peninsula. Visit his website at www.johnstaugustine.com.

HAMPTON ROADS

PUBLISHING COMPANY, INC.

Thank you for reading *Living an Uncommon Life*. Hampton Roads is proud to publish an extensive array of books on the topics discussed in this book, such as unlocking your potential, the power of mind, prosperity, and more. Please take a look at the following selections and visit us anytime on the web: www.hrpub.com.

Excuse Me, Your Life Is Waiting
The Astonishing Power of Feelings
Lynn Grabhorn

Ready to get what you want? Get this, hard work and positive thinking can't do it alone. Lynn Grabhorn introduces you to "The Law of Attraction" and uncovers the hidden power of positive feeling. Now in paperback, this upbeat yet down-to-earth book reveals how our true feelings work to "magnetize" and create the reality we experience.

Discover the secrets that have made *Excuse Me* a *New York Times* bestseller!

Paperback • 328 pages • ISBN 1-57174-381-2 • $16.95

BeliefWorks
The Art of Living Your Dreams
Ray Dodd

In this practical guide to reprogramming the core beliefs that drive your daily decision making, Dodd reveals how our beliefs are constructed and offers techniques for transforming self-limiting beliefs and unlocking the door to the life you desire.

"When you change what you believe, you change your story about yourself, and suddenly life becomes a beautiful dream. *BeliefWorks* will show you how."
—don Miguel Ruiz, author of *The Four Agreeements*

Paperback • 200 pages • ISBN 1-57174-472-X • $14.95